CBEST Reading Practice Tests
Expanded Edition

CBEST Test Preparation
Reading Study Guide for the
California Basic Educational Skills Test

CBEST Reading Practice Tests Expanded Edition: CBEST Test Preparation Reading Study Guide for the California Basic Educational Skills Test

ISBN: 978-1-949282-72-6

For information on bulk discounts, please contact Exam SAM via our webpage.

TABLE OF CONTENTS

Format of the CBEST Reading Test

Two types of reading skills are assessed on the CBEST reading test:

(1) Critical Analysis and Evaluation

(2) Comprehension and Research

Type 1 Questions

Critical analysis and evaluation questions assess your understanding of the specific details within a reading selection or selections.

Critical analysis and evaluation questions also cover understanding the author's purpose, technique, or assumptions, as well as making comparisons and predictions.

Type 2 Questions

Comprehension questions cover the logical organization of the reading selection.

This means that you will see questions on the relationship of ideas within a text, as well as having to identify the main idea or draw inferences.

Research questions assess understanding tables of contents, as well as comprehending data that is represented in tables, charts, or graphs.

Types of Questions on the CBEST Reading Test

You will see these specific types of questions on the CBEST reading test:

(1) CRITICAL ANALYSIS AND EVALUATION

- Comparing and contrasting ideas within a reading selection or selections

- Identifying details that support the author's main idea

- Predicting an outcome based on information from a selection

- Understanding the author's viewpoint or attitude

- Determining the relevance of ideas to a selection

- Recognizing arguments for or against a viewpoint

- Understanding the author's persuasive techniques or strategies

- Identifying the author's purpose or assumptions

- Discerning facts from opinions in a selection

- Identifying inconsistencies or differences between two or more paragraphs or selections

- Recognizing the intended audience for a selection

- Identifying the tone or style of writing

(2) COMPREHENSION AND RESEARCH SKILLS

- Identifying and understanding relationships between general and specific ideas in a selection

- Determining the correct order of events or of steps in a process

- Arranging ideas logically within a selection

- Recognizing the main idea of a selection

- Paraphrasing and summarizing ideas in selections

- Drawing conclusions and making generalizations

- Recognizing implications and making inferences

- Determining the meaning of unknown words or metaphorical phrases

- Identifying varying interpretations of words or information in a selection

- Understanding the relationship between meaning and context

- Using key transition and linking words correctly within a selection

- Understanding the organizational schemes of various selections

- Understanding how to use the table of contents or index of a selected book to locate information

- Identifying the place where specific information is located within a book

- Using and interpreting information in tables, graph, or charts

How to Use This Study Guide

The reading practice tests in this study guide contain questions of all of the types that you will see on the real CBEST test.

Practice test 1 in this book is in "tutorial mode."

As you complete practice test 1, you should pay special attention to the tips highlighted in the special boxes.

Although you will not see tips like this on the actual exam, these suggestions will help you improve your performance on each subsequent practice test in this publication.

You should also study the explanations to the answers to practice test 1 especially carefully.

Studying the tips and explanations in reading practice test 1 will help you obtain strategies to improve your performance on the other practice tests in this book.

Of course, these strategies will also help you do your best on the day of your actual CBEST test.

CBEST Practice Reading Test 1

Look at the extract from an index below to answer the two questions that follow.

Light   20–45

    beams 29

    bulbs 30–41

        energy-saving 40–41

        florescent 32–33

        halogen 36–39

        incandescent 30–31

        neon 34–35

    emission of   20–23

    emitting diode 27, 29

    speed of   24–26

        measuring 24–25

        physics 26

    waves 28

Lightning   93–96

    causes of 93

    surviving strikes of 95

1.   What method best describes the organization of the section on light bulbs?

    A. by date

    B. by popularity

    C. by energy consumption

    D. by cost per bulb

    E. by type

2.   Where can the reader look to see whether the book contains information on how the emission of light is measured?

    A. Pages 27 and 29

    B. Pages 20–23

    C. Pages 24–25

    D. Page 26

    E. Page 28

Questions 1 and 2 are research skills questions.
Question 1 assesses your understanding of how to use an index, while question 2 covers the skill of identifying where specific information is located within a book.

Tips and Explanations:

1. The correct answer is E. Using an index or table of contents correctly requires you to understand the organizational scheme of the sections within the table of contents or index. You need to look at the information in each section and then ask yourself what the items within the section have in common. We can see that the section on light bulbs is organized by

type of light bulb because energy-saving, florescent, halogen, incandescent, and neon are different kinds of light bulbs.

2. The correct answer is B. When questions ask you to identify where specific information is located within a book, you need to read through each part of the table of contents or index. The indentation of each section is extremely important for these types of questions. For instance, look at this excerpt from the index:

Lightning   93–96
        causes of 93

The indented item always relates to the category above. So, the causes of lighting are discussed on page 93. Our question is asking us about the measurement of the emission of light. Based on the indentations, the reader can look at pages 20 to 23 to see whether the book contains information on how the emission of light is measured. Remember to be very careful when considering the indentation in the index. Pages 20–23, on line 9 of the index, deal with the emission of light, although if you misread the index, line 9 looks like it deals with the emission from bulbs.

Read the passage below and answer the four questions that follow.

Research shows that the rise in teenage smoking over the last ten years took place primarily in youth from more affluent families, in other words, families in which both parents were working and earning good incomes. Therefore, these teenagers were not from disadvantaged homes, as most people seemed to believe.

The facts demonstrate quite the opposite because the most striking and precipitous rise in smoking has been for teenagers from the most financially advantageous backgrounds. Furthermore, because of various lawsuits against the major tobacco companies, the price of cigarettes has actually declined sharply over the past decade. The paradox is that the increased demand for cigarettes originated from new teenage smokers who were from well-off families. Yet, contrary to these market forces, the price of tobacco products fell during this time.

3.   What is the primary purpose of this passage?
      A. to provide information on a recent trend
      B. to emphasize the dangers of smoking
      C. to dispel a common misconception
      D. to highlight the difference between two types of teenagers
      E. to criticize teenage smokers

4.   Which of the following is the best meaning of the word precipitous as it is used in this passage?
      A. unreliable
      B. unbelievable
      C. predictable

D. dangerous

E. dramatic

5. From this passage, it seems safe to conclude which of the
    following?

    A. The majority of new teenage smokers in the last ten years could
       have afforded to pay higher prices for tobacco.

    B. Parents of affluent families are often not aware of the smoking
       habits of their children.

    C. Smoking among teenagers from disadvantaged homes also
       increased during the past decade.

    D. Major tobacco companies have recently faced bankruptcy.

    E. There has been a rise in smoking cessation programs for
       teenagers during the past decade.

6. Which of the following statements gives the best summary of the
    main points of the lecture?

    A. Teenagers from affluent families smoke more than teenagers
       from disadvantaged homes.

    B. The price of tobacco products is normally unrelated to market
       forces.

    C. The price of cigarettes has fallen more than expected during the
       last ten years.

    D. Contrary to popular belief, the rise in teenage smoking during
       the last ten years has been attributable to youth from wealthy
       family backgrounds.

    E. There has been a noticeable increase in teenage smoking in
       recent years.

> Question 3 is a critical analysis question on the author's purpose.
> Question 4 is a comprehension question on the meaning of unknown words.
> Question 5 is a comprehension question on drawing conclusions.
> Question 6 is an example of a question that asks you to summarize information from a passage.

Tips and Explanations:

3. The correct answer is C. In order to determine the author's purpose, you need to pay special attention to the last sentence of the first paragraph of a selection. This is where the writer normally puts his or her thesis statement, which is the author's main assertion or primary purpose. Looking at the last sentence of the first paragraph, we can see that the primary purpose of this passage is to dispel a common misconception. The idea of a misconception is indicated in the phrase "as most people seem to believe" from the last sentence of the first paragraph.

4. The correct answer is E. For questions on the meaning of words, you need to look for other words in the passage that are synonyms for the word in the question. "Dramatic" and "precipitous" are synonyms in the context of this passage. The word "striking" from the first sentence of the second paragraph of the passage is also a synonym for "precipitous."

5. The correct answer is A. When drawing conclusions, look for words and phrases in the passage that express the writer's viewpoint. See the phrase "contrary to these market forces" in the last sentence of the passage. The market forces refer to the factors that would have caused the price of

tobacco to increase. Based on the word "contrary," it seems safe to conclude that the majority of new teenage smokers in the last ten years could have afforded to pay higher prices for tobacco, but in spite of this fact, the price did not go up.

6. The correct answer is D. For questions asking you to summarize the main points, you first must identify what the main points are. Paragraph 1 states that there has been a recent misconception about teenage smoking. Paragraph 2 explains that the price of tobacco should have gone up because youngsters from wealthy families could have afforded to pay a higher price. The following statement gives the best summary of the main points of the lecture because it mentions the misconception, as well as the pricing aspect: "Contrary to popular belief, the rise in teenage smoking in the last ten years has been attributable to youth from wealthy family backgrounds." So, answer D is the best summary of this paragraph.

Read the passage below and answer the three questions that follow.

Over the past five years, sales of organic products in the United States have increased a staggering 20 percent, with retail sales per year of more than 9 billion dollars. American farmers have realized that organic farming is an incredibly cost-effective method because it can be used to control costs, _____ to appeal to higher-priced markets.

Organic farming has become one of the fastest growing trends in agriculture recently not only for monetary, but also for environmental reasons. _____ the monetary benefits, organic farming also results in positive ecological outcomes. That is because the use of chemicals and synthetic materials is strictly prohibited.

7.   Which of the words or phrases, if inserted in order into the blanks in the passage, would help the reader better understand the sequence of events?

    A. besides; As a result of

    B. as well as; Apart from

    C. while; In addition to

    D. in addition; However

    E. but also; Considering

8.   Which sentence or phrase from the passage best expresses its central idea?

    A. Over the past five years, sales of organic products in the United States have increased a staggering 20 percent, with retail sales per year of more than 9 billion dollars.

B. American farmers have realized that organic farming is an incredibly cost-effective method because it can be used to control costs.

C. Organic farming has become one of the fastest growing trends in agriculture recently not only for monetary, but also for environmental reasons.

D. Organic farming also results in positive ecological outcomes.

E. That is because the use of chemicals and synthetic materials is strictly prohibited.

9.   What word best describes the style of writing in this passage?

A. commercial

B. technical

C. scientific

D. explanatory

E. polemical

Question 7 is a comprehension question on using key transition and linking words.
Question 8 is a comprehension question on recognizing the main idea.
Question 9 is an example of a question on identifying the style of writing in a selection.

Tips and Explanations:

7. The correct answer is B. For questions on transition and linking words, look carefully at the information that is provided in the selection after the gap. Determine whether an additional supporting idea is being stated or if the author is changing the subject. Then look at the answer choices to see

which one matches the flow of the text. "As well as" is the most suitable answer for the first gap in this selection because another reason is being given. "Apart from" fits best into the second gap because ecological outcomes are mentioned, in addition to the environmental reasons.

8. The correct answer is C. For main idea questions, look to see which ideas are stated in each part of the selection. In the selection above, the first half of the passage addresses economics, while the second half talks about the environment. The central idea of the passage is therefore that organic farming has become one of the fastest growing trends in agriculture recently not only for monetary, but also for environmental reasons. This is the only answer that expresses both of the ideas. The other answers are merely restating specific points from the selection.

9. The correct answer is D. In order to identify the style of a selection, you need to examine the transitional words and phrases in the passage. We can see that reasons and explanations are given in the passage, using the phrases "not only," "but also," and "that is because." Accordingly, the writing style is explanatory.

Read the passage below and answer the three questions that follow.

The corpus of research on Antarctica has resulted in an abundance of factual data. For example, we now know that more than ninety-nine percent of the land is completely covered by snow and ice, making Antarctica the coldest continent on the planet. This inhospitable climate has brought about the adaptation of a plethora of plants and biological organisms present on the continent. Investigations into the sedimentary geological formations provide testimony to the process of adaptation. Sediments recovered from the bottom of Antarctic lakes, as well as bacteria discovered in ice, have been of invaluable significance because they have revealed the history of global climate change over the past 10,000 years.

10. According to the passage, the plants and organisms in Antarctica:
    A. have survived because of the process of adaptation.
    B. are the result of sedimentary geological formations.
    C. cover more than 99% of the land surface.
    D. grow in the bottom of lakes on the continent.
    E. reveal the history of climate change over the past 10,000 years.

11. The information the writer conveys in this passage is addressed mainly to:
    A. professional geologists.
    B. tourists taking part in a trip to Antarctica.
    C. elementary school children.
    D. researchers prior to an expedition.
    E. students attending a college lecture.

12. Which one of the following statements best expresses the writer's opinion regarding the corpus of research on Antarctica?

    A. It was exceptionally difficult due to the snow and ice coverage on the ground.

    B. It provides us with more accurate information on colder climates.

    C. It has helped us better to understand historical climatic fluctuations in the rest of the world.

    D. It reveals important data on organisms typically found in lakes.

    E. It is linked to changes in world history.

For the selection above, we have three types of critical analysis and evaluation questions.

Question 10 is a critical analysis question on identifying details from a passage.

Question 11 is a critical analysis question that asks you to recognize the intended audience for the selection.

Question 12 is an evaluation asking you to understand the author's viewpoint.

Tips and Explanations:

10. The correct answer is A. For questions on identifying details from the passage, you need to locate precise information within the selection. You can do this by using keywords. Looking at question 10, we can see that we are required to find specific details about plants and organisms. The keywords "plants" and "organisms" are mentioned in the third sentence of the passage, which states: "This inhospitable climate has brought about the adaptation of a plethora of plants and biological organisms present on

the continent." Answer A also mentions the process of adaption, so it is the correct answer.

11. The correct answer is E. When you have to identify the intended audience, you should evaluate the vocabulary that the passage uses. In this selection, we see words such as "research," "data," and "testimony." Then ask yourself: Who uses this type of vocabulary? Words like these are too academic for tourists or children, but not technical enough for professionals or researchers. Therefore, we know that the audience for selection consists of students attending a college lecture.

12. The correct answer is C. In order to understand the author's viewpoint, you need to look for adjectives. Words such as "important," "helpful," or "significant" will be in the selection if the writer has a positive viewpoint. If the writer is expressing a negative viewpoint, you will see adjectives such as "pointless" or "useless." In our selection, the answer is found in the last sentence of the passage in the phrase ". . . have been of invaluable significance because they have revealed the history of global climate change." The phrase "invaluable significance" reveals the author's positive view of the research, while the phrase "the history of global climate change" is synonymous with "historical climatic fluctuations in the rest of the world."

Read the passage below and answer the two questions that follow.

[1]The student readiness educational model is based on the view that students operate at different levels of ability. [2]For some students, this might mean that they are operating above the average ability level of their contemporaries. [3]Other students may be functioning at a level that is below average. [4]Of course, students in a particular class may be of slightly different ages. [5]There are also students who are at the optimum learning level. [6]The level is optimum because they are being challenged and learning new things, but they do not feel overwhelmed or inundated by the new information. [7]A teacher will engage students best with classroom learning activities that are fun and interesting.

13. Which numbered sentence provides an opinion rather than a fact?
    A. Sentence 1
    B. Sentence 2
    C. Sentence 5
    D. Sentence 6
    E. Sentence 7

14. Which numbered sentence is least relevant to the main idea of the passage?
    A. Sentence 2
    B. Sentence 3
    C. Sentence 4
    D. Sentence 5
    E. Sentence 6

Question 13 is an evaluation question asking you to discern facts from opinions.

Question 14 is another evaluation question. It requires you to determine the relevance of ideas to the selection.

Tips and Explanations:

13. The correct answer is E. Opinion questions are similar to viewpoint questions, which we have seen previously in question 12. For these types of questions, you need to look for adjectives that the author uses. Here, we can see that sentence 7 is an opinion, not a fact. Sentence 7 states: "A teacher will engage students best with classroom learning activities that are fun and interesting." The adjective "best" indicates that an opinion is being given.

14. The correct answer is C. For relevancy questions, you should again look at the vocabulary. Try to determine if there is any word or idea that is being repeated in the majority of the sentences in the selection. In the selection above, we can see that the word "level" is used in the majority of sentences in the passage. Age is a different concept than level. So, sentence 4, which states that students in a particular class may be of slightly different ages, is least relevant to the main idea of the passage. In other words, we know from reading the passage that slight differences in ages should not affect the teaching or learning processes.

Use the graph below to answer the question that follows.

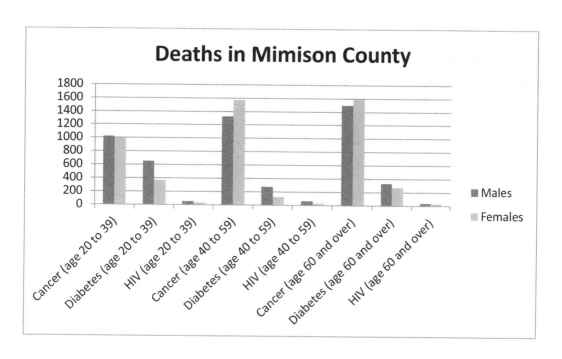

15. Which group in total had the highest number of deaths from all three diseases (cancer, diabetes, and HIV)?

A. Males, age 20 to 39

B. Females, age 20 to 39

C. Males, age 40 to 59

D. Females, age 40 to 59

E. Females, age 60 and over

> Question 15 is a research skills question that requires you to interpret information from a chart or graph. In this case, we have to evaluate a bar graph.

Tips and Explanations:

15. The correct answer is E. For these types of questions, you need to look at the data in the chart or graph, and then visually evaluate the information for each group in total. For the graph above, first look at the groups of dark grey bars, which represent males. Then look at the light grey bars, which are for the female population. You will see that all of the light grey bars for the 40 to 59 group are slightly lower than those of the 60 and over group. We can also clearly see that the first light grey bar in the age 60 and over group is the highest one of any of the bars. Adding this first light grey bar for cancer at 1,600 to the 220 for diabetes and the 20 for HIV, we arrive at 1,840 in total for all three diseases for females over age 60, which is the highest number of deaths from all three diseases.

Read the passage below and answer the four questions that follow.

Earthquakes occur when there is motion in the tectonic plates on the surface of the earth. The crust of the earth contains twelve such tectonic plates. Fault lines, the places where these plates meet, build up a great deal of pressure because the plates are always pressing on each other. The two plates will eventually shift or separate because the pressure on them is constantly increasing, and this build-up of energy needs to be released. When the plates shift or separate, we have an occurrence of an earthquake, also known as a seismic event.

The point where the earthquake is at its strongest is called the epicenter. Waves of motion travel out from this epicenter, often causing widespread destruction to an area. With this likelihood for earthquakes to occur, it is essential that earthquake prediction systems are in place. _____ _____ .

However, these prediction systems need to be more reliable in order to be of any practical use.

16. What happens immediately after the pressure on the tectonic plates has become too great?
    A. Fault lines are created.
    B. There is a build-up of energy.
    C. There is a seismic event.
    D. Waves of motion travel out from the epicenter.
    E. Prediction systems become more reliable.

17. Which sentence, if inserted into the blank line in paragraph 2, would best fit into the logical development of the passage?

A. Unfortunately, many countries around the world do not have earthquake prediction systems.

B. The purpose of earthquake prediction systems is to give advanced warning to the population, thereby saving lives in the process.

C. Earthquakes can also occur at sea since there are tectonic plates in certain oceans.

D. It is extremely costly to rectify the destruction that earthquakes cause.

E. Aftershocks can also occur after the tremors of the earthquake have passed.

18. What inference about earthquakes can be drawn from the passage?

A. There has been no discernible change in the number of earthquakes in recent years.

B. There has been an increase in the destruction caused by earthquakes in recent years.

C. The destruction of property could be avoided with improved earthquake prediction systems.

D. The number of deaths from earthquakes could be lowered if earthquake prediction systems were more reliable.

E. Earthquake prediction systems could help to lessen the strength of earthquakes.

19.   The writer makes her final statement more compelling by preceding
       it by which of the following?

       A. a dispassionate, scientific explanation

       B. emotionally-evocative examples

       C. a historical account of events

       D. a prediction of a future catastrophe

       E. step-by-step instructions

Question 16 is the type of comprehension question that asks you to determine the correct order of events or steps in a process.

Question 17 is another type of comprehension question. It requires you to arrange ideas logically within a selection.

Question 18 is another example of a comprehension question. It requires you to draw an inference.

Question 19 is a type of critical analysis question. It asks you to understand the author's persuasive technique or strategies.

Tips and Explanations:

16. The correct answer is C. For questions asking you about the order of steps or events, you need to focus on the part of the selection where the particular step is mentioned. Here, we can see that the question is asking about the occurrence of pressure on the tectonic plates. So, we need to focus on the last two sentences of the first paragraph: "The two plates will eventually shift or separate because the pressure on them is constantly increasing, and this build-up of energy needs to be released. When the plates shift or separate, we have an occurrence of an earthquake, also

known as a seismic event." You also need to pay attention to the words in the question that are indicating the sequencing, such as "before," "after," "next," or "during." The question asks us: "What happens immediately *after* the pressure on the tectonic plates has become too great?" The word "after" shows that we need to determine the next step. The selection indicates that after the pressure builds up, it needs to be released. The passage states that the release of energy in this way causes an earthquake, which is also called "a seismic event." So, answer C is correct.

17. The correct answer is B. In order to arrange ideas within a selection, pay special attention to the sentences before and after the gap. The sentence before the gap and the sentence after the gap both talk about earthquake prediction systems, so the sentence that goes in the gap should also mention this topic. By process of elimination, we can exclude answers C, D, and E because these three answers mention earthquakes only in general, but not prediction systems in particular. Answer B is the best answer because it mentions saving lives, which relates to the practical use of the prediction systems, mentioned in the last sentence.

18. The correct answer is D. In order to draw an inference, you should make only a small logical step based on the information contained in the selection. Try to avoid making wild guesses. In this selection, we see that the sentence to be placed in the gap mentions that lives can be saved through prediction systems, while the last sentence states that "these prediction systems need to be more reliable in order to be of any practical use." Accordingly, we can surmise that at the time the selection was

written, prediction systems were not reliable enough. Therefore, not as many lives were being saved as would have been possible if the systems had been more reliable.

19. The correct answer is A. For questions about the author's persuasive technique or strategies, you should focus on the sentences before the one that contains the final direct statement by the author. In the selection above, the author's final direct statement is that "these prediction systems need to be more reliable in order to be of any practical use." The author's final statement is dispassionate because she precedes it with the scientific descriptions of earthquake waves and epicenters. [Note that "dispassionate" means objective or stated without strong emotion.]

Read the passage below and answer the two questions that follow.

In December 406 AD, departing from what is now called Germany, 15,000 warriors crossed the frozen Rhine River and traveled into the Roman Empire of Gaul. A new historical epoch would soon be established in this former Roman Empire.

Even though this period has diminished in historical significance in comparison to more recent events, the demise of the Roman Empire in the fifth century was certainly unprecedented. Today, the collapse of the Roman Empire remains significant because it marks the commencement of what we now call the Middle Ages, the six subsequent centuries that followed the demise of Roman rule.

20.   According to the passage, the Roman Empire:

A. was established during the Middle Ages.

B. is now referred to as Germany.

C. gradually collapsed throughout the Middle Ages.

D. fell into ruin from 406 to 499 AD.

E. has become more historically significant in recent times.

21.   Which of the following outlines best describes the organization of the topics addressed in paragraphs I and II?

A. I. Invasion of Germany in the fifth century; II. A comparison to recent current events

B. I. Background to the Middle Ages; II. The demise of the Roman Empire

C. I. Crossing the Rhine River for battle; II. Historical significance of the collapse of the Roman Empire

D. I. A new historical epoch for the Roman Empire; II. Why the Roman Empire collapsed

E. I. The invasion of the Roman Empire of Gaul; II. The beginning of the Middle Ages

> Question 20 is the type of comprehension question that requires you to understand the relationship between general and specific ideas in a selection.
> Question 21 is the type of comprehension question that asks you to understand the organizational scheme of a selection.

Tips and Explanations:

20. The correct answer is D. Be sure to look at the relationship between the general idea and the specific points for questions like this one. From the selection, we can see that the general idea is the history of the Roman Empire and that the specific ideas are the dates of the events. From the first sentence, we know that the Roman Empire of Gaul was invaded in 406. In the second paragraph, we read that the Roman Empire fell into demise in the fifth century, which is the 100-year period ending in 499 AD. Therefore, we can conclude that the Roman Empire fell into ruin from 406 to 499 AD.

21. The correct answer is E. For questions on organizational scheme like this one, you have to be careful that the answer is not too specific. In other words, you should normally try to choose the most general answer, without choosing an overgeneralization. Paragraph one of the passage talks about warriors crossing the frozen Rhine River and traveling into the Roman Empire of Gaul. Therefore, paragraph one focuses on the invasion of the Roman Empire of Gaul. Paragraph two explains that the Roman Empire remains significant because it marks the commencement (or beginning) of what we now call the Middle Ages.

Read the passage below and answer the three questions that follow.

American Major League Baseball consisted of only a handful of teams when the National League was founded in 1876. Yet, baseball has grown in popularity <u>by leaps and bounds</u> over the years.

This growth in popularity resulted in increased ticket sales for games and bolstered the profits of its investors. The increased demand from the public, in turn, precipitated the formation of a new division, known as the American League, in 1901.

Additionally, new teams have been formed from time to time in accordance with regional demand. This was the case with the Colorado Rockies in Denver, Colorado, and the Tampa Bay Rays in Tampa Bay, Florida.

22.   The main purpose of the passage is:
   A. to give examples of some popular American baseball teams.
   B. to provide step-by-step information about the process of forming new baseball teams.
   C. to trace historical developments relating to the popularity of baseball.
   D. to criticize Americans who depend on baseball for entertainment.
   E. to compare and contrast the American and National Baseball Leagues.

23. Which one of the following phrases is closest in meaning to <u>by leaps and bounds</u> as it is used in the above text?

A. with unbelievable speed

B. by exceeding the boundaries

C. with sporadic movements

D. contrary to public opinion

E. surpassing all requirements

24. Which of the following assumptions has influenced the writer?

A. The increase in ticket sales is a direct result of increased investment.

B. Those who invest money in baseball teams make too much profit from their investment.

C. New baseball teams are more popular than established teams.

D. The popularity of American baseball will continue to increase steadily in the future.

E. The formation of baseball teams is based on certain economic principles.

> Question 22 is another critical analysis question on the author's purpose. We have seen one of these types of questions previously at number 3 above.
> Question 23 is the type of comprehension question that requires understanding the relationship between meaning and context.
> Question 24 is a critical analysis and evaluation question on identifying the author's assumptions.

Tips and Explanations:

22. The correct answer is C. Remember that in order to determine the author's purpose, you need to pay special attention to the last sentence of the first paragraph of a selection. This is where the author normally puts his or her thesis statement. From the phrase "over the years" in the author's thesis statement, we know that the passage has a historical focus. The selection begins with the founding date of 1876, moves on to a major event in 1901, and finishes by talking about more recent developments. So, the main purpose of the passage is to trace historical developments relating to the popularity of baseball. You may be tempted to choose answer B. However, the passage is not systematic enough to be classified as a step-by-step description.

23. The correct answer is A. This question requires that you understand the relationship between meaning and context. For these types of questions, you need to look in the selection for phrases that are synonyms or antonyms to the phrase in the question. The phrase "by leaps and bounds" is an idiomatic expression which refers to something that happens very quickly or dramatically. This is in contrast to the phrase "only a handful of teams" from the first sentence of the selection.

24. The correct answer is E. In order to identify the author's assumptions, you should evaluate the phrases that the author uses to expand his or her assertions. In the selection above, we can see that the author mentions that baseball's popularity "bolstered the profits of its investors." Additionally, the last paragraph states that "new teams have been formed from time to time in accordance with regional demand." Profit and demand

are two economic concepts, so we can conclude that the formation of baseball teams is based on certain economic principles.

Read the passage below and answer the three questions that follow.

Airline travel is generally considered to be an extremely safe mode of transportation. Indeed, statistics reveal that far fewer individuals are killed each year in airline accidents than in crashes involving automobiles. _____ this safety record, airlines deploy ever-increasingly strict standards governing the investigation of aircraft crashes. Information gleaned from the investigation of aircraft crashes is important _____ it is utilized in order to prevent such tragedies from occurring again in the future.

25.   Which one of the following statements is not supported by information contained in the passage?

   A. Airline crash investigation standards have become more rigorous.
   B. It is safer to travel in an airplane than in a car, according to the statistics.
   C. Traveling by air is normally very safe.
   D. Data from airline accidents is used to make improvements to airline safety standards.
   E. The number of airline accidents has decreased in recent years.

26. Which of the words or phrases, if inserted in order into the blanks in the passage, would help the reader better understand the sequence of events?

A. Besides; as a result

B. In spite of; because

C. In addition to; although

D. Apart from; while

E. Despite; due to

27. Who is the writer's audience?

A. a group of young children

B. college students attending a lecture

C. the general public

D. pilots on a training program

E. key members of airline staff

Question 25 is a critical analysis and evaluation question that requires you to compare and contrast the ideas stated in the question to those within the selection.
Question 26 is another question on using key transition and linking words, like question 7 above.
Question 27 is a question on the author's intended audience. We have seen this question type before at number 11 above.

Tips and Explanations:

25. The correct answer is E. For questions that require you to compare and contrast the ideas stated in the question to the ideas stated within the selection, you should use the process of elimination technique. Answer A is stated in the passage because the adjective "rigorous" from the answer is synonymous with the phrase "ever-increasingly strict standards" from sentence three of the passage. The information from answers B and C is stated in the second sentence of the passage. The information from answer D is stated in the last sentence of the passage. Answer E is not stated in the passage. The final sentence mentions the hope that accidents will decline in the future, but we do not know if this is in fact the case.

26. The correct answer is B. Remember that for questions on transition and linking words, you need to look carefully at the information that is provided in the selection after the gap. Determine whether an additional supporting idea is being stated or if the author is changing the subject. "In spite of" fits in the first gap because there is a shift in tone from the idea of safety to the idea of accident prevention. "Because" fits in the second gap since there is a cause-and-effect relationship between acquiring the information and preventing the accidents.

27. The correct answer is C. Remember that in order to identify the intended audience, you should evaluate the vocabulary that the passage uses. The information in the passage is pitched to an audience of general members of the public. The vocabulary used in the passage is too advanced for a group of young children, while it is not sufficiently

academic for college students attending a lecture. The information is not technical enough for pilots on a training program or for key members of airline staff.

Read the passage below and answer the three questions that follow.

Clones have been used for centuries in the field of horticulture. For instance, florists have traditionally made clones of geraniums and other plants by modifying cuttings and re-planting them in fresh soil. As a result, cloning is considered acceptable and predictable in the realm of plants and flowers.

However, the rapid development of science and technology means that cloning processes could now be used on humans. _____ _____ .

This fear stems from the ethical ramifications that will inevitably occur if cloning is extended to the human species.

28.   From the information in this passage, it is reasonable to infer that:
    A. The subject of cloning has become somewhat controversial recently.
    B. Cloning has fallen out of favor with horticulturalists.
    C. In spite of certain misgivings, many people support human cloning.
    D. Technological advances have impeded the use of cloning.
    E. Cloning on human beings could be used for positive purposes.

29. Which sentence, if inserted into the blank line in paragraph 2, would be most suitable for the author's audience and purpose?

    A. Dolly the sheep was an early example of how cloning could be successfully used on mammals.

    B. But human cloning and horticultural cloning are worlds apart.

    C. Many people believe that the cloning of human beings has sinister undertones.

    D. That is why scientists need to have reservations in this area.

    E. Clones are not exactly like those that we see in the movies.

30. Between paragraphs 1 and 2, the writer's approach shifts from:

    A. cause to effect

    B. problem to solution

    C. explanation to example

    D. approbation to misgivings

    E. advantages to disadvantages

Question 28 is the type of question that asks you to make an inference. We have seen this type of question previously at number 18 above.
Question 29 is another question on arranging ideas within a selection, like question 17 above.
Question 30 is a further type of question on organizational schemes of selections, like question 21 above.

Tips and Explanations:

28. The correct answer is A. You will recall that in order to draw an inference, you should make only a small logical step based on the

information contained in the selection. In the selection above, we can understand that the topic is controversial because the first paragraph states that "cloning is considered acceptable and predictable in the realm of plants and flowers." However, the second paragraph qualifies this statement by countering that there is a "fear [that] stems from the ethical ramifications" of using the process on humans.

29. The correct answer is C. For questions on arranging ideas within a selection, you have to pay special attention to the sentences before and after the gap. Here, we need a sentence that will link the idea of using cloning on humans, which is mentioned the first sentence, to the idea of the fears surrounding human cloning, which is stated in the last sentence. Sentence C does this because it contains the synonymous phrases "the cloning of human beings" [i.e., the idea of using cloning on humans] and "sinister undertones" [i.e., the idea of the fears surrounding human cloning].

30. The correct answer is D. Remember that for questions on organizational scheme, you have to be careful that the answer is not too specific. "Approbation" means approval. The idea of approbation sums up the first paragraph because it states that cloning is approved for horticultural uses. "Misgivings" means fears or concerns, such as the fears about the ethical considerations of human cloning, which are considered in the second paragraph. You may be tempted to choose answer E. However, the ethical considerations are more than a mere disadvantage since they bring fear along with them.

Read the passage below and answer the four questions that follow.

Working in a run-down laboratory near Paris, Marie Curie worked around the clock to discover a radioactive element. When she finally captured her quarry in 1902, she named it "radium" after the Latin word meaning ray.

Madame Curie should certainly be an inspiration to scientists today. She had spent the day blending chemical compounds which could be used to destroy unhealthy cells in the body. As she was about to retire to bed that evening, she decided to return to her lab. There she found that the chemical compound had become crystalized in the bowls and was emitting the elusive light that she sought.

Inspired by the French scientist Henri Becquerel, Curie won the Nobel Prize for Chemistry in 1903. Upon winning the prize, she declared that the radioactive element would be used only to treat disease and would not be used for commercial profit.

Today radium provides an effective remedy for certain types of cancer. Radium, now used for a treatment called radiotherapy, works by inundating diseased cells with radioactive particles. Its success lies in the fact that it eradicates malignant cells without any lasting ill effects on the body.

31. Which of the following is the best meaning of the word <u>quarry</u> as it is used in this passage?

    A. a precious commodity

    B. an unknown catalyst

    C. an object that is sought

    D. a chemical compound

    E. a source that emits light

32. According to the information in the passage, why is radium treatment used as a cancer therapy?

    A. because it is cost effective

    B. because it destroys cancerous cells

    C. because it has no long-term effects

    D. because it emits a glowing light

    E. because it derives from a radioactive element

33. What is the most appropriate title of the passage?

    A. Madame Curie: An Inventive Chemist

    B. The Discoveries of Madame Curie

    C. The Use of Radium to Treat Cancer

    D. Madame Curie: A Brief Biography

    E. The Discovery and Use of Radium

34. Which of the following phrases or sentences from the passage expresses an opinion rather than a fact?

    A. Marie Curie worked around the clock to discover a radioactive element.

    B. Madame Curie should certainly be an inspiration to scientists today.

C. She had spent the day blending chemical compounds which could be used to destroy unhealthy cells in the body.

D. Upon winning the prize, she declared that the radioactive element would be used only to treat disease and would not be used for commercial profit.

E. Today radium provides an effective remedy for certain types of cancer.

Question 31 is a comprehension question that asks you to identify varying interpretations of a word.
Question 32 is like question 10 above. It is asking you to identify details from the selection.
Question 33 is asking you to find the title for the selection. This is another type of main idea question, like question 8 above.
Question 34 is like number 13 above. It is asking you to discern facts from opinions.

Tips and Explanations:

31. The correct answer is C. For vocabulary questions like this one, you need to bear in mind that the word provided will have different interpretations, depending on its context. "Quarry" can mean a hole in which one digs for rock. Alternatively, "quarry" can refer to something that is hunted or pursued. Also remember that for vocabulary questions, you need to look for synonyms in the passage. In sentence one, we see the word "discover." In the last sentence of paragraph two, we see the phrase "the elusive light that she sought." Therefore, we can surmise that "quarry" is something one wants to discover or an object being sought.

32. The correct answer is B. Be careful. Questions like this will have distractor answers which will reiterate phrases from the passage, although these phrases do not answer the question. We know that answer B is correct because the final sentence of the passage states: "Its success lies in the fact that it eradicates malignant cells without any lasting ill effects on the body." You may be tempted to choose answer C. However, answer C is too general since radium has long-term positive effects [i.e., destroying malignant cells] without having any long-term negative effects.

33. The correct answer is E. For main idea questions, as well as for questions on selecting a title for a selection, you will need to choose an answer that is neither too general nor too specific. Answers A, B, and D are much too general since the passage does not focus on the entire life and work of Madame Curie. Answer C is too specific because cancer treatment is mentioned in only the last paragraph. Therefore, "The Discovery and Use of Radium" is the best title for the passage.

34. The correct answer is B. For "opinion vs. fact" questions like this, look for modal verbs (should, would, may, might) and superlative adjectives that express opinions (the best, the most, etc). The notion whether someone should be an inspiration to others is a matter of personal opinion, so B is the best answer. You may be tempted to choose answer E. However, the adjective "effective" is factually qualified by the use of the phrase "certain types."

Read the passage below and answer the three questions that follow.

In Southern Spain and France, Stone Age artists painted stunning drawings on the walls of caves nearly 30,000 years ago. Painting pictures of the animals upon which they relied for food, the artists worked by the faint light of lamps that were made of animal fat and twigs.

In addition to having to work in relative darkness, the artists had to endure great physical discomfort since the inner chambers of the caves were sometimes less than one meter in height. Thus, the artists were required to crouch or squat uncomfortably as they practiced their craft.

Their paints were mixed from natural elements such as yellow ochre, clay, calcium carbonate, and iron oxide. However, many other natural elements and minerals were not used. An analysis of the cave paintings reveals that the colors of the paints used by the artists ranged from light yellow to dark black.

The artists utilized ochre and manganese as engraving tools in order first to etch their outlines on the walls of the caves. Before removing their lamps and leaving their creations to dry, they painted the walls with brushes of animal hair or feathers. Archeologists have also discovered that ladders and scaffolding were used in higher areas of the caves.

35. What was the last step in the process of Stone Age cave drawings?

    A. The paintings were etched.

    B. The paint was applied.

    C. The lamps were removed.

    D. The artwork was left to dry.

    E. The scaffolding was erected.

36. Which of the following best expresses the attitude of the writer?

    A. It is surprising that the tools of Stone Age artists were similar to those that artists use today.

    B. It is amazing that Stone Age artists were able to paint such beautiful creations in spite of the extreme conditions they faced.

    C. The lack of light in the caves had an effect on their esthetic quality.

    D. It is predictable and banal that Stone Age artists would paint pictures of animals.

    E. The use of natural elements in paint was not an environmentally-friendly practice.

37. Which sentence is least relevant to the main idea of the passage?

    A. Thus, the artists were required to crouch or squat uncomfortably as they practiced their craft.

    B. Their paints were mixed from natural elements such as yellow ochre, clay, calcium carbonate, and iron oxide.

    C. However, many other natural elements and minerals were not used.

D. An analysis of the cave paintings reveals that the colors of the paints used by the artists ranged from light yellow to dark black.

E. The artists utilized ochre and manganese as engraving tools in order first to etch their outlines on the walls of the caves.

Question 35 asks you to determine the correct order of events or steps in a process, like question 16 above. Question 36 is like question 12 above. It is an evaluation question on understanding the author's viewpoint. Question 36 asks you to determine the relevance of ideas to the selection, like question 14 above.

Tips and Explanations:

35. The correct answer is D. We need to have a look at the first and second sentences of the last paragraph, which state: "The artists utilized ochre and manganese as engraving tools in order first to etch their outlines on the walls of the caves. Before removing their lamps and leaving their creations to dry, they painted the walls with brushes of animal hair or feathers." Be sure to read sentences like this one very carefully. The etching is the first step. The application of the paint is the second step. Removing the lamps is the third step, while leaving the paint to dry is the final step.

36. The correct answer is B. The attitude of the writer is that it is amazing that Stone Age artists were able to paint such beautiful creations in spite of the extreme conditions they faced. For questions like this one, look for adjectives in the passage that give hints about the author's point of view.

The phrase "stunning drawings" in paragraph one indicates the author's amazement.

37. The correct answer is C. The article focuses on the natural elements that were used in the process of creating the drawings. The passage is therefore not concerned with other natural elements that were not used.

Look at the table of contents below from an introductory textbook on computer science in order to answer the two questions that follow.

38. Which part of the book is most likely to address the care and maintenance of computer equipment?

A. Introduction

B. Part 1

C. Part 2

D. Part 3

E. Part 4

39. Where can the reader find the names of the people and organizations that the author has thanked for their support during the writing of the book?

A. Acknowledgments

B. Introduction

C. Recommendations

D. Bibliography

E. Index

> Question 38 and 39 are similar to questions 1 and 2 above. However, here we are asked to evaluate a table of contents, rather than an index.

Tips and Explanations:

38. The correct answer is C. The care and maintenance of computer equipment would be discussed in Part 2 since computer equipment is synonymous with hardware.

39. The correct answer is A. "Acknowledge" means to recognize as important or to thank, so the names of the people and organizations that the author has thanked for their support during the writing of the book would appear in the acknowledgments section.

Read the passage below and answer the four questions that follow.

The world's first public railway carried passengers, even though it was primarily designed to transport coal from inland mines to ports on the North Sea. Unveiled on September 27, 1825, the train had 32 open wagons and carried over 300 people.

The locomotive steam engine was powered by what was termed the steam-blast technique. _____
_____ . In this way, the steam created a draft of air which followed after it, creating more power and speed for the engine.

The train had rimmed wheels which ran atop rails that were specially designed to give the carriages a faster and smoother ride. While the small carriages could hardly be termed <u>commodious</u>, the locomotive could accelerate to 15 miles per hour, a record-breaking speed at that time.

Subsequently, the inventor of the locomotive, George Stephenson, revolutionized his steam engine by adding 24 further pipes. Now containing 25 tubes instead of one, Stephenson's second "iron horse" was even faster and more powerful than his first creation.

40. Which of the following is the best meaning of the word commodious as it is used in this passage?

A. small

B. uncomfortable

C. spacious

D. speedy

E. smooth

41. Which sentence, if inserted into the blank line in paragraph 2, would best fit into the logical development of the passage?

A. The chimney of the locomotive redirected exhaust steam into the engine via a narrow pipe.

B. This technique was quite innovative at that time, making Stephenson its pioneer.

C. Previous engines had used different propulsion devices that were not as powerful.

D. Most of the passengers were unaware of the technology behind Stephenson's invention.

E. Because of the power of the engine, it was important to ensure that the passengers would have a smooth ride.

42. Why was the second locomotive that Stephenson invented an improvement on his first?

A. because it ran more smoothly

B. because it was more comfortable

C. because it could carry more passengers

D. because it contained more pipes and tubes

E. because it ran with greater force and speed

43. From the information contained in the passage, it seems reasonable to infer which of the following?

A. Many passengers were frightened about traveling on Stephenson's new locomotive.

B. George Stephenson's inventions laid the basic foundations for modern day public trains and railways.

C. Profits in the coal industry increased after the invention of the locomotive.

D. Stephenson should have been able to invent a locomotive that could run faster.

E. Stephenson's second locomotive carried more passengers than his first one.

Question 40 is another comprehension question on the meaning of unknown words.
Question 41 is the type of question that requires to you to arrange ideas logically within a selection.
Question 42 a critical analysis question on identifying details from the passage.
Question 43 is an example of a comprehension question that requires you to draw an inference.

Tips and Explanations:

40. The correct answer is C. Remember that for vocabulary questions like this one, you will need to look for synonyms or antonyms of the word in question. The sentence begins "While the small carriages could hardly be termed commodious . . ." so we know that the word "commodious" is the opposite of small. Accordingly, "spacious" is the correct answer.

41. The correct answer is A. When placing a sentence into a gap in a paragraph, you need to look carefully at the sentences before and after the gap in order to discover what idea unites the paragraph. In this case, the idea of steam, specifically the movement of steam, is mentioned in both of these two sentences. Sentence A also talks about the movement of steam, so it is the best answer.

42. The correct answer is E. The last sentence of the paragraph states that "Stephenson's second 'iron horse' was even faster and more powerful than his first creation." In other words, we can conclude that the second locomotive was an improvement because it ran with greater force and speed that the first one did.

43. The correct answer is B. The passage describes how George Stephenson invented the steam locomotive and the world's first public railway. Such inventions lay the basic foundations, which can later be improved upon with advances in technology. So, George Stephenson's inventions laid the basic foundations for modern day public trains and railways.

Read the passage below and answer the three questions that follow.

Highly concentrated radioactive waste is lethal and can remain so for thousands of years. Accordingly, the disposal of this material remains an issue in most energy-producing countries around the world. In the United States, for example, liquid forms of radioactive waste are usually stored in stainless steel tanks. For extra protection, the tanks are double-walled and surrounded by a concrete covering that is one meter thick. This storage solution is also utilized the United Kingdom, in most cases.

The long-term problem lies in the fact that nuclear waste generates heat as radioactive atoms decay. This excess heat could ultimately result in a radioactive leak. Therefore, the liquid needs to be cooled by pumping cold water into coils inside the tanks. However, the tanks are only a temporary storage solution. The answer to the long-term storage of nuclear waste may be fusing the waste into glass cylinders that are stored deep underground.

44.   How are the tanks which are used for storing radioactive waste protected against leaks?

    A. They are encased in concrete.

    B. They only contain waste in liquid form.

    C. They provide a place where radioactive atoms can decay.

    D. They are combined with cold water.

    E. They are fused into glass cylinders.

45. Which of the following outlines best describes the organization of the topics addressed in paragraphs I and II?

A. I. Radioactive Waste in the US and UK; II. Storage Problems

B. I. Current Storage Solutions for Radioactive Waste; II. Potential Problems and Long-Term Solutions

C. I. Radioactive Waste: The Long-Term Risks; II. Looking for Potential Solutions

D. I. The Threat of Radioactive Waste; II. The Creation of Glass Cylinders

E. I. Stainless Steel Storage Tanks for Radioactive Waste; II. The Generation of Heat and Potential for Leaks

46. Which of the following assumptions has most influenced the writer?

A. The threat of a radioactive leak is exaggerated by the public.

B. The storage of radioactive waste in stainless steel tanks is extremely dangerous.

C. The United Kingdom normally follows practices that the United States has adopted.

D. The underground storage of glass cylinders containing radioactive waste is going to be a very risky procedure.

E. A radioactive leak would have disastrous consequences around the globe.

Question 44 is a critical analysis question on identifying details from the passage.
Question 45 is the type of comprehension question that asks you to understand the organizational scheme of a selection.
Question 46 a critical analysis and evaluation question on identifying the author's assumptions.

Tips and Explanations:

44. The correct answer is A. The tanks are protected against leaks because they are encased in concrete. The fourth sentence of paragraph one states: "For extra protection, the tanks are double-walled and surrounded by a concrete covering that is one meter thick."

45. The correct answer is B. The first two sentences of paragraph one introduce the idea of radioactive waste generally, before moving on to talk about how the waste is stored at the present time, so the best title for paragraph one is "Current Storage Solutions for Radioactive Waste." Paragraph two begins by discussing the problems with storing the waste in this way and ends by giving an overview of possible solutions to these problems, so "Potential Problems and Long-Term Solutions" is the best title for paragraph two.

46. The correct answer is E. The author implies that a radioactive leak would have dire consequences since he opens the passage with this sentence: "Highly concentrated radioactive waste is lethal and can remain so for thousands of years."

Read the passage below and answer the four questions that follow.

Best known for his process of pasteurization, or the <u>eradication</u> of germs in liquid substances, Louis Pasteur was also the father of the modern rabies vaccine. In December of 1880, a friend who was a veterinary surgeon gave Pasteur two rabid dogs for research purposes.

Victims of bites from rabid dogs normally showed no symptoms for three to twelve weeks. By then, however, the patient would be suffering from convulsions and delirium, and it would be too late to administer any remedy. Within days, the victim would be dead.

So-called treatments at that time consisted of burning the bitten area of skin with red-hot pokers or with carbolic acid. _____ _____ . Pasteur devoted himself to discovering a more humane and effective method of treatment for the disease.

His tests on rabid dogs confirmed that the rabies germs were isolated in the saliva and nervous systems of the animals. After many weeks of tests and experiments, Pasteur at last cultivated a vaccine from a weakened form of the rabies virus itself.

47. Which sentence, if inserted into the blank line in paragraph 3, would be most appropriate for the author's audience and purpose?
    A. These "remedies" often resulted in fatal trauma to the patients.
    B. Carbolic acid was also a common cleaning agent at that time.
    C. Dog owners were often unaware that their pets were infected with rabies.

D. As medical professionals, you are aware of the dangers of these types of "treatments."

E. Researchers today continue to cultivate new strains of the rabies vaccine.

48. Which of the following is the best meaning of the word <u>eradication</u> as it is used in this passage?

A. cleansing

B. reduction

C. destruction

D. amelioration

E. assuagement

49. What are the symptoms of rabies infection, if it is left untreated?

A. reddening of the skin

B. burning sensation of the skin

C. seizures and anxiety

D. muscular contractions and forgetfulness

E. mental disturbances and physical tremors

50. What is the most appropriate title of this passage?

A. Pasteurization and the Rabies Vaccine

B. The Life and Work of Louis Pasteur

C. Pasteur's Discovery of the Rabies Vaccine

D. Experimental Research on Rabid Dogs

E. Uses of the Modern Rabies Vaccine

Question 47 is another type of question on the author's intended audience.
Question 48 is another vocabulary question.
Question 49 is another identifying details question.
Question 50 is a further question on finding the title for a selection.

Tips and Explanations:

47. The correct answer is A. This paragraph is devoted to discussing how patients used to be treated for rabies. Sentence A is the only option that talks about patients, so it is the best answer.

48. The correct answer is C. The sentence states: "Best known for his process of pasteurization, or the eradication of germs in liquid substances, Louis Pasteur was also the father of the modern rabies vaccine." Common sense tells us that germs are something negative that we would want to get rid of permanently, so "destruction" is the best answer. "Amelioration" and "assuagement" both mean to lessen the intensity of something, not to get rid of it permanently, so they are not the best answers.

49. The correct answer is E. Paragraph two states: "Victims of bites from rabid dogs normally showed no symptoms for three to twelve weeks. By then, however, the patient would be suffering from convulsions and delirium, and it would be too late to administer any remedy." "Delirium" means mental disturbances and "convulsions" means physical tremors.

50. The correct answer is C. The passage talks mostly about how Pasteur discovered the rabies vaccine, so "Pasteur's Discovery of the Rabies

Vaccine" is the best title. You may be tempted to choose answer A. However, pasteurization is mentioned only in passing. Answer B is an overgeneralization. Answers D and E are too specific.

CBEST Practice Reading Test 2

Look at the extract from an index below to answer the two questions that follow.

1. Which page gives information about what determines whether a person is called "an inventor"?

    A. 138

    B. 139

    C. 140

    D. 141

    E. 157

2. How is the section of the book on individual inventors organized?

    A. alphabetically by inventor's last name

    B. chronologically by date of invention

    C. from the most to least significant

    D. by nationality of inventor

    E. by categories of use

Read the passage below and answer the three questions that follow.

Cancer occurs when cells in the body begin to divide abnormally and form more cells without control or order. There are some factors which are known to increase the risk of cancer. Smoking is the largest single cause of death from cancer in the United States. _____ , poor food choices increase cancer risk. Indeed, research shows that there is a definite link between the consumption of high-fat food and cancer.

If a cell divides when it is not necessary, a large growth called a tumor can form. These tumors can usually be removed, and in many cases, they do not come back. _____ , in some cases the cancer from the original tumor spreads. The spread of cancer in this way is called metastasis.

There are some factors which are known to increase the risk of cancer. Smoking is the single largest cause of death from cancer in the United States. One-third of the deaths from cancer each year are related to smoking, making tobacco use the most preventable cause of death in this country.

3. Which of the words or phrases, if inserted in order into the blanks of the passage, would help the reader better understand the sequence of events?

A. However; Yet

B. Although; Therefore

C. Also; Thus

D. Moreover; Even though

E. In addition; However

4. What inference can be drawn from this passage?

A. A low-fat diet can reduce the risk of cancer.

B. The consumption of high-fat food has increased in recent years.

C. Most cancer sufferers have made poor food choices.

D. Smoking always causes cells to divide abnormally.

E. The number of people who smoke is bound to decrease in the future.

5. What is metastasis?

A. the abnormal growth of organs

B. when a tumor begins to grow in size

C. the growth of cancer in a cell

D. the growth of cancer inside a tumor

E. the spread of cancer from a tumor

Read the passage below and answer the three questions that follow.

The theory of multiple intelligences (MI) is rapidly replacing the intelligence quotient, or IQ. The IQ, long considered the only valid way of measuring intelligence, has come under criticism recently because it inheres in many cultural biases. For this reason, there has been a movement away from the IQ test, which is now seen as an indication of a person's academic ability. On the other hand, the theory of multiple intelligences measures practical skills such as spatial, visual, and musical ability.

Howard Gardner, the researcher who designed the system of multiple intelligences, <u>posits</u> that while most people have one dominant type of intelligence, most of us have more than one type. Of course, that's why they are known as multiple intelligences. As we will see today, this theory has important implications for teaching and learning.

6.   Which of the following groups of statements best summarizes the main topics addressed in each paragraph?

    A. I. Disadvantages of the IQ test; II. The work of Howard Gardner

    B. I. The rise of the theory of multiple intelligences; II. Further information on the theory of multiple intelligences

    C. I. Cultural biases of the IQ test; II. The plurality of multiple intelligences

    D. I. IQ testing and academic performance; II. Dominant types of multiple intelligences

    E. I. The various aspects of multiple intelligences; II. Multiple intelligences in teaching and learning

7.   Which of the following is the best meaning of the word <u>posits</u> as it is used in this passage?

   A. says

   B. points out

   C. suggests

   D. postulates

   E. considers

8.   The information the writer conveys in this passage is addressed mainly to:

   A. licensed psychologists attending a conference.

   B. college students attending a psychology class.

   C. college students attending an education class.

   D. the general public.

   E. young children.

Read the passage below and answer the two questions that follow.

Around the world today, more than a billion people still do not have fresh, clean drinking water available on a daily basis. Hundreds of thousands of people in developing countries die needlessly every year because of the consumption of unclean, disease-ridden water. In brief, fresh water saves lives. However, what has been understood only recently is that in order to improve the global water supply, those who manage water supplies must evaluate in more detail how developed countries consume their available drinking water. Without this evaluation, an ever-increasing number of individuals will continue to die from water-related diseases.

9.   We can conclude from the information in this passage that:

A. water-related disease will decline in the future.

B. the majority of water-related deaths could be avoided.

C. children are the most vulnerable to water-related disease and death.

D. developing countries manage their water supplies better than developed countries.

E. governments will intervene to manage the world's water supplies.

10.   Which of the following assumptions has influenced the writer?

A. Developing countries are culpable for the pollution of their own drinking water.

B. The provision of fresh drinking water is the most pressing problem in recent current events.

C. The consumption of water in developed countries could serve as a model to other countries.

D. People living in developing countries should know better than to consume polluted water.

E. The political climate of developing countries impedes their ability to have fresh drinking water.

Read the passage below and answer the four questions that follow.

In his first mathematical formulation of gravity, published in 1687, Sir Isaac Newton posited that the same force that kept the moon from being propelled away from the earth also applied to gravity at the earth's surface. While this finding, termed the Law of Universal Gravitation, is said to have been occasioned by Newton's observation of the fall of an apple from a tree in the orchard at his home, in reality the idea did not come to the scientist in <u>a flash of inspiration</u>, but was developed slowly over time.

It is because of Newton's work that we currently understand the effect of gravity on the earth as a global system. As a result of Newton's investigation into the subject of gravity, we know today that geological features such as mountains and canyons can cause variances in the earth's gravitational force. Newton must also be acknowledged for the realization that the force of gravity becomes less robust as the distance from the equator diminishes, due to the rotation of the earth, as well as the declining mass and density of the planet from the equator to the poles.

11. What is the author's main purpose?
     A. to analyze natural phenomena
     B. to reconcile various gravitational theories
     C. to identify a reservation which Newton experienced
     D. to emphasize the significance of Newton's achievement
     E. to give background about Newton's life

12. Which of the following phrases is closest in meaning to the phrase a flash of inspiration as it is used in the above text?

A. in hindsight

B. with trepidation

C. all of a sudden

D. with clarity

E. little by little

13. What is the pattern of organization of the passage?

A. cause and effect

B. general to specific

C. explanation and example

D. historical background and current applications

E. theoretical development and new innovations

14. Which of the following is a factor in the diminishment of the force of gravity when one is closer to the equator?

A. Because the relative weight of the Earth is higher in this particular geographical location

B. Because the Earth's gravitational force has changed positions

C. Because one is further from geographical features such as mountains and canyons

D. Because the way in which the Earth rotates is different near the equator

E. Because the distance to the poles has decreased

Read the passage below and answer the two questions that follow.

In the Black Hills, four visages protrude from the side of a mountain. The faces are those of four pivotal United States' presidents: George Washington, Thomas Jefferson, Theodore Roosevelt, and Abraham Lincoln. Washington was chosen on the basis of being the first president. Jefferson was selected because he was instrumental in the writing of the American Declaration of Independence. Lincoln was selected on the basis of the mettle he demonstrated during the American Civil War and Roosevelt for his development of Square Deal policy, as well as being a proponent of the construction of the Panama Canal.

15. From this passage, it seems reasonable to infer that these four presidents were chosen because:
    A. of their outstanding courage.
    B. their faces would be esthetically sympathetic to the natural surroundings.
    C. they helped to improve the national economy.
    D. they were considered the most popular among members of the public.
    E. their work was considered crucial to the progress of the nation.

16. Which of the following is the best meaning of the word mettle as it is used in this passage?
    A. emotion
    B. courage
    C. persistence
    D. persuasion
    E. determination

Use the graph below to answer the question that follows.

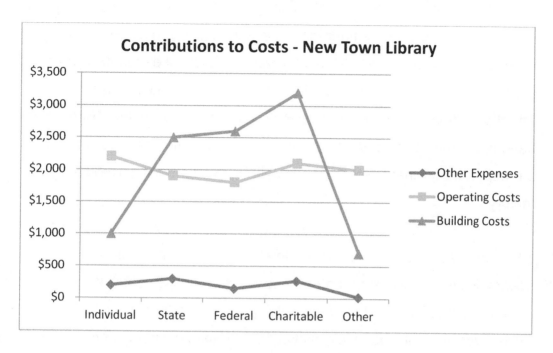

Contributions to Costs - New Town Library

17. Which source provides the greatest amount of funding for the combined total of all three of the above types of costs?

    A. Private

    B. State

    C. Federal

    D. Charitable

    E. Other

Read the passage below and answer the three questions that follow.

[1]Socio-economic status, rather than intellectual ability, may be the key to a child's success later in life. [2]Consider two hypothetical elementary school students named John and Paul. [3]Both of these children work hard, pay attention in the classroom, and are respectful to their teachers. [4]Both boys have the same hobbies and musical tastes. [5]Nevertheless, Paul's father is a prosperous business tycoon, while John's has a menial job working in a factory.

[6]Despite the similarities in their academic aptitudes, the disparate economic situations of their parents means that Paul is nearly 30 times more likely than John to land a high-flying job by the time he reaches his fortieth year. [7]In fact, John has only a 12% chance of finding and maintaining a job that would earn him even a median-level income. [8]This outcome is inherently unfair because economic rewards should be judged by and distributed according to the worthiness of the employment to society as a whole, rather than according to social status or prestige.

18. What is the writer's primary persuasive technique?
   A. quoting from authorities
   B. appealing to emotion
   C. refuting opposing viewpoints
   D. predicting future consequences
   E. using statistical evidence

19. Which numbered sentence provides an opinion rather than a fact?

    A. Sentence 1

    B. Sentence 3

    C. Sentence 5

    D. Sentence 7

    E. Sentence 8

20. Which numbered sentence is least relevant to the main idea of the first paragraph?

    A. Sentence 1

    B. Sentence 2

    C. Sentence 3

    D. Sentence 4

    E. Sentence 5

Read the passage below and answer the three questions that follow.

The Hong Kong and Shanghai Bank Corporation (HSBC) skyscraper in Hong Kong is one of the world's most famous high-rise buildings. The building was designed so that it had many pre-built parts that were not constructed on site. This prefabrication made the project a truly international effort: The windows were manufactured in Austria, the exterior walls were fabricated in the United States, the toilets and air-conditioning were made in Japan, and many of the other components came from Germany.

The HSBC tower consists of 47 stories, which is an immense contrast to the twenty-story buildings in its vicinity. In fact, the previous buildings constructed on this site were limited by the soft and often water-logged ground in the surrounding area. _____ _____ . This assessment was necessary in order to ensure that subsidence, and potential collapse of the new structure, could be averted.

21. Which sentence, if inserted into the blank line in paragraph two, would best fit into the logical development of the passage?

    A. Water-logging is a common problem in construction projects of this type.

    B. Many occupants of the neighboring buildings objected to the construction of the new skyscraper.

    C. For this reason, the groundwater supply had to be carefully assessed prior to construction of the HSBC building.

    D. Therefore, the new skyscraper was bound to dominate its structurally smaller neighbors.

    E. Subsidence is the phenomenon that occurs when a building shifts from its original position.

22. Which statement below best represents the writer's opinion?

    A. Prefabricated buildings are more international than those built on site.

    B. Countries should work together more often in construction projects.

    C. Careful planning is paramount for construction projects in urban settings.

    D. The HSBC building is well-known because many countries were involved in its construction.

E. Construction projects should not disturb the natural groundwater supply.

23. Between paragraphs 1 and 2, the writer's approach shifts from:

A. scientific detail to current problems

B. interesting facts to potential problems

C. analytical background to public inquiry

D. explanation to example

E. cause to effect

Read the passage below and answer the two questions that follow.

The study of philosophy usually deals with two key problem areas: human choice and human thought. A consideration of these problem areas is not an aspect of psychology or art. The first problem area, human choice, asks whether human beings can really make decisions that can change their futures. Conversely, it also investigates to what extent the individual's future is fixed and pre-determined by cosmic forces outside the control of human beings. In the second problem area, human thought, epistemology is considered. "Epistemology" means the study of knowledge; it should not be confused with ontology, the study of being or existence.

24. The primary purpose of the passage is:

A. to compare two areas of an academic discipline.

B. to explain key aspects of the work of a particular philosopher.

C. to contrast psychological and artistic views on a particular topic.

D. to investigate two troublesome aspects of human behavior.

E. to provide historical background on the subject of philosophy.

25. Which sentence does not fit with the logical flow of the paragraph?

   A. A consideration of these problem areas is not an aspect of psychology or art.

   B. The first problem area, human choice, asks whether human beings can really make decisions that can change their futures.

   C. Conversely, it also investigates to what extent the individual's future is fixed and pre-determined by cosmic forces outside the control of human beings.

   D. In the second problem area, human thought, epistemology is considered.

   E. "Epistemology" means the study of knowledge; it should not be confused with ontology, the study of being or existence.

Read the passage below and answer the four questions that follow.

In the fall of 1859, a discouraged man was sitting in his run-down law office in Springfield, Illinois. He was fifty years old, in debt, and had been a lawyer for twenty years, earning on average 3,000 dollars a year. This man would later go on to do great things for his country. His name was Abraham Lincoln.

_____ these obvious financial constraints, some of Abraham Lincoln's associates had already begun to put forward the idea that he should run for president of the United States. Lincoln began to write influential Republican Party leaders for their assistance. By 1860, Lincoln had <u>garnered</u> more public support, after having delivered public lectures and political speeches in various states. _____ he was the underdog, Lincoln won 354 of the 466 total nominations at the Republican National Convention and was later elected President of the United States.

26. Which of the words or phrases, if inserted in order into the blanks of the passage, would help the reader better understand the sequence of events?
    A. Despite; As a result of
    B. Although; In spite of
    C. With; Even though
    D. During; Being
    E. In spite of; Although

27. Which of the following outlines best describes the organization of the topics addressed in paragraphs I and II?
    A. **I.** Lincoln's profession as a lawyer; **II.** Why Lincoln was the underdog
    B. **I.** Lincoln's life in Springfield; **II.** Lincoln's speeches and conventions
    C. **I.** Lincoln's biographical information; **II.** Lincoln's campaign and election
    D. **I.** Lincoln's financial problems; **II.** Lincoln's campaign advisors
    E. **I.** Lincoln's future achievement; **II.** How Lincoln won the election

28. Which of the following is the best meaning of the word <u>garnered</u> as it is used in this passage?

   A. taken

   B. earned

   C. forced

   D. achieved

   E. financed

29. Which of the following assumptions has influenced the writer?

   A. Successful politicians often encounter financial problems.

   B. A career in law provides a good background for a career in politics.

   C. Lincoln was an unlikely presidential candidate.

   D. Lincoln had an enduring legacy on the history of the United States.

   E. In order to win an election, a candidate must first obtain the support of his or her party.

Read the passage below and answer the three questions that follow.

The use of computers in the stock market helps to control national and international finance. These controls were originally designed in order to create long-term monetary stability and protect shareholders from catastrophic losses. Nevertheless, because of the high level of automation now involved in buying and selling shares, computer-to-computer trading could result in a downturn in the stock market.

Such a slump in the market, if not properly regulated, could bring about a computer-led stock market crash. _____ _____ . For this reason, regulations have been put in place by NASDAQ, AMEX, and FTSE.

30.   Which sentence, if inserted into the blank line in the passage, would best fit with the author's audience and purpose?

    A. Bonds and pension plans are also secure long-term investments.

    B. Trading shares via the internet has certainly increased nowadays.

    C. So be sure you frequently change the password you use for trading online.

    D. Needless to say, such an economic collapse would have disastrous consequences for the entire nation.

    E. The computer is an efficient tool for stock brokers as well, despite the risks.

31. Which sentence from the passage best expresses its central idea?

A. The use of computers in the stock market helps to control national and international finance.

B. These controls were originally designed in order to create long-term monetary stability and protect shareholders from catastrophic losses.

C. Nevertheless, because of the high level of automation now involved in buying and selling shares, computer-to-computer trading could result in a downturn in the stock market.

D. Such a slump in the market, if not properly regulated, could bring about a computer-led stock market crash.

E. For this reason, regulations have been put in place by NASDAQ, AMEX, and FTSE.

32. Based on the information contained in the passage, what is a likely conclusion regarding computer-to-computer trading?

A. Therefore, computer-to-computer trading is usually regarded as being safer now than it has been in the past.

B. The volume of computer-to-computer trading is likely to decrease in the future because of the controls that have been introduced.

C. Accordingly, the government needs to act now in order to introduce further controls on computer-to-computer trading.

D. Hence, the fees charged by stockbrokers are bound to increase.

E. Personal trading of shares via the internet will become more popular in the future.

Read the passage below and answer the four questions that follow.

Good nutrition is essential for good health. A healthy diet can help a person to maintain a good body weight, promote mental wellbeing, and reduce the risk of disease. So, you might ask, what does healthy nutrition consist of? Well, first of all, a healthy diet should include food from all of the major food groups. These food groups are carbohydrates, fruit, vegetables, dairy products, meat and other proteins, and fats and oils.

Besides this, it is also important to try to avoid processed or convenience food. Packaged food often contains chemicals, such as additives to enhance the color of the food or preservatives that give the food a longer life. Food additives are <u>deleterious</u> to health for a number of reasons. First of all, they may be linked to disease in the long term. In addition, they may block the body's ability to absorb the essential vitamins and minerals from food that are required for healthy bodily function.

33. What is the most appropriate title for this passage?
     A. Good Health and Wellbeing
     B. How to Eat a Balanced Diet
     C. The Dangers of Food Additives
     D. The Risks of Food Preservatives
     E. The Basics of Healthy Nutrition

34. Who is most likely to be the audience of this passage?

    A. Adults listening to a radio program on nutrition

    B. Medical doctors attending a seminar

    C. Participants in a weight-loss support group

    D. College students in a biology lecture

    E. Young children in an elementary school assembly

35. Which of the following words is closest in meaning to the word deleterious as it is used in the passage?

    A. insipid

    B. harmful

    C. impeding

    D. provoking

    E. preventative

36. According to the passage, what is the primary reason why manufacturers of processed food use additives?

    A. to make food more convenient

    B. to improve the appearance of the food

    C. to prevent the food from spoiling quickly

    D. to add nutrients to the food

    E. to remove harmful chemicals from the food

Read the passage below and answer the two questions that follow.

Although there are many different types and sizes of coins in various countries, vending machines around the world operate on the same basic principles.

The first check is the slot: coins that are bent or too large will not go in. Once inside the machine, coins fall into a cradle which weighs them. If a coin is too light, it is rejected and returned to the customer.

Coins that pass the weight test are then passed along a runway beside a magnet. Electricity passes through the magnet, causing the coin to slow down in some cases. If the coin begins to slow down, its metallurgic composition has been deemed to be correct.

The coin's slow speed causes it to miss the next obstacle, the deflector. Instead, the coin falls into the "accept" channel and the customer receives the product.

37.   Based on the information in the passage, how is the metallurgical composition of a coin determined to be correct?
    A. By its weight
    B. By its increased velocity in the runway
    C. By whether it runs alongside the magnet
    D. By the electricity that has passed through the magnet
    E. By missing the deflector

38. The last step in testing the coin is:

A. the slot

B. determination of metallurgic composition

C. the accept channel

D. the deflector

E. the customer's receipt of the product

Look at the table of contents below from an astronomy textbook in order to answer the two questions that follow.

39. The reader wants to see if this textbook has made any reference to another book entitled: *The Earth and the Sky*. Where can the reader look to determine this the most quickly?

    A. Part 1

    B. Part 2

    C. List of Terms

    D. Bibliography

    E. Index

40. Which part of the book is most likely to discuss whether inter-planetary space travel will be undertaken in the future?

    A. Part 1

    B. Part 2

    C. Part 3

    D. Part 4

    E. Index

Read the passage below and answer the three questions that follow.

Michelangelo began work on the painting of the ceiling of the Sistine Chapel in the summer of 1508, assisted by six others who helped to mix his paint and plaster. However, as work proceeded, the artist dismissed each of his assistants one by one, claiming that they lacked the competence necessary to do the task at hand.

Described as the lonely genius, the painter himself often felt incompetent to complete the project entrusted to him by Pope Julius II. Having trained as a sculptor, Michelangelo had an extremely low opinion of his own painting skills. Yet, he went on to paint one of the most beautiful works in art history.

In spite of his frequent personal misgivings, he persevered to paint the ceiling with his vision of the creation of the universe. _____ _____ . The scenes include the Separation of Light from Darkness, the Drunkenness of Noah, the Ancestors of Christ, and the Salvation of Mankind.

41.   Which sentence below, if inserted into the blank in the last paragraph, would be most consistent with the logical flow of the passage?

A. The nine scenes that he created ran in a straight line along the ceiling.

B. He was originally commissioned to paint portraits of the twelve apostles.

C. The Pope also had some misgivings about Michelangelo.

D. People in the Vatican had grown accustomed to seeing the painter looking tired and disheveled.

E. Michelangelo preferred to work alone and without distraction.

42. Why did Michelangelo dismiss his assistants?

A. Because he decided that he preferred to mix his plaster by himself.

B. Because their dismissal was requested by the Pope.

C. Because he believed that they were inept craftsmen.

D. Because he felt incompetent about his own abilities.

E. Because they had no training in sculpture.

43. Which of the sentences from the passage, repeated below, expresses an opinion of the author rather than a fact?

A. However, as work proceeded, the artist dismissed each of his assistants one by one, claiming that they lacked the competence necessary to do the task at hand.

B. Described as the lonely genius, the painter himself often felt incompetent to complete the project entrusted to him by Pope Julius II.

C. Having trained as a sculptor, Michelangelo had an extremely low opinion of his own painting skills.

D. Yet, he went on to paint one of the most beautiful works in art history.

E. In spite of his frequent personal misgivings, he persevered to paint the ceiling with his vision of the creation of the universe.

Read the passage below and answer the four questions that follow.

The pyramids at Giza in Egypt are still among the world's largest structures, even today. The monuments were constructed well before the wheel was invented, and it is notable that the Egyptians had only the most primitive, handmade tools to complete the massive project.

Copper saws were used to cut softer stones, as well as the large wooden posts that levered the stone blocks into their final places. Wooden mallets were used to drive flint wedges into rocks in order to split them. An instrument called an adze, which was similar to what we know today as a wood plane, was employed to give wooden objects the correct finish.

The Egyptians also utilized drills that were fashioned from wood and twine. In order to ensure that the stones were level, wooden rods were joined by strips of twine to check that the surfaces of the stone blocks were flat. Finally, the stone blocks were put onto wooden rockers so that they could more easily be placed into their correct positions on the pyramid.

44. The two tools which were used to place the stones into their final positions on the pyramid were made from which substance?
    A. flint
    B. copper
    C. twine
    D. stone
    E. wood

45. Between paragraphs 1 and 2, the writer's approach shifts from:

A. scientific explanation to technical analysis

B. reasoned argument to impassioned persuasion

C. background information to specific details

D. personal opinion to justification

E. cause to effect

46. What is the writer's main purpose?

A. to give a step-by-step explanation of the construction of the Giza pyramids

B. to compare the construction of the Giza pyramids to that of modern day structures

C. to give an overview of some of the main implements that were used to construct the Giza pyramids

D. to highlight the importance of the achievement of the construction of the Giza pyramids

E. to bring to light a misconception in previous accounts of the construction of the Giza pyramids

47. Which of the following assumptions has most influenced the writer?

A. It is incredible that the Egyptians were able to construct the pyramids using only hand-made tools.

B. It is a pity that the wheel was not available to the Egyptians during the construction of the pyramids at Giza.

C. Modern construction projects could learn from the example of the Giza pyramids.

D. The most difficult aspect of the project was placing the stones in the correct position on the pyramid.

E. The pyramids could have been larger if more modern tools had been available.

Read the passage below and answer the three questions that follow.

She sighed in despair as he again showed no capacity to change his ways. "Why can't he see reason?" she wondered silently to herself for the umpteenth time that day.

The baby whimpered futilely in the next room, amid piles of unworn and unloved clothing. He too had learned that no matter how fiercely he cried, no one would come to his aid.

At times she felt like challenging her husband more strongly, or at least asking for an explanation of his behavior. Sadly, she too had been conditioned to learn that such actions were <u>inutile</u>. So, mute and hopeless, she stoically faced another day of domestic misery.

48. Which sentence from the passage best expresses its central idea?

A. She sighed in despair as he again showed no capacity to change his ways.

B. The baby whimpered futilely in the next room, amid piles of unworn and unloved clothing.

C. He too had learned that no matter how fiercely he cried, no one would come to his aid.

D. At times she felt like challenging her husband more strongly, or at least asking for an explanation of his behavior.

E. Sadly, she too had been conditioned to learn that such actions were useless.

49. What is the best meaning of the word <u>inutile</u> as it is used in the passage?

A. helpless

B. useless

C. impertinent

D. desperate

E. unimportant

50. Which word below best describes the woman's behavior to her spouse?

A. amiable

B. accustomed

C. relentless

D. futile

E. resigned

ANSWER KEY AND EXPLANATIONS

Practice Reading Test 2

1. The correct answer is D. On line 5 of the index, you will see that page 141 gives the definition of the word "inventor."

2. The correct answer is A. The index mentions Edison, Marconi, and Singer in that order, so they are organized alphabetically by last name.

3. The correct answer is E. The gap in paragraph 2 introduces a second factor, so the phrase "in addition" is suitable. "However" is best for the second gap because there is a change in point of view, shifting from the idea that tumors can be removed to the idea that tumors sometimes spread.

4. The correct answer is A. The inference that a low-fat diet can reduce the risk of cancer can be drawn from this passage. The reverse of this idea is provided in the last sentence of the first paragraph, which states that "research shows that there is a definite link between the consumption of high-fat food and cancer."

5. The correct answer is E. Metastasis is the spread of cancer from a tumor. This idea is supported by the last two sentences of the second paragraph: "in some cases the cancer from the original tumor spreads. The spread of cancer in this way is called metastasis."

6. The correct answer is B. Paragraph 1 discusses the increase in popularity of the theory of multiple intelligences, while paragraph 2 gives

further information on the theory of multiple intelligences, namely, some background information and a discussion of the educational implications. Therefore, answer B is the best because it is gives the general ideas of each paragraph. The other answers give only specific ideas from each of the paragraphs.

7. The correct answer is D. The words "posit" and "postulate" describe how theories are formed.

8. The correct answer is C. The last sentence talks about implications for teaching and learning, so the talk is being given in an education class.

9. The correct answer is B. We can conclude from the information in this passage that the majority of water-related deaths could be avoided. This idea is supported by the phrase "die needlessly" in the second sentence of the passage.

10. The correct answer is C. The assumption that has influenced the writer is that the consumption of water in developed countries could serve as a model to other countries. This is idea supported by the second to the last sentence in the passage, which mentions evaluating water management in developed countries: "what has been understood only recently is that in order to improve the global water supply, those who manage water supplies must evaluate in more detail how developed countries consume their available drinking water."

11. The correct answer is D. The author's main purpose is to emphasize the significance of Newton's achievement. This is supported by paragraph

2 sentence 1: "It is because of Newton's work that we currently understand the effect of gravity on the earth as a global system."

12. The correct answer is C. The phrase "flash of inspiration" means all of a sudden. The text gives the opposite idea at the end of the first paragraph, when it states that Newton's theories "developed slowly over time."

13. The correct answer is D. The pattern of organization of the passage is historical background in paragraph 1 and current applications in paragraph 2. The passage begins by talking about the year 1687, and then signals that it is moving to current applications by using the word "currently" in the first sentence of the second paragraph.

14. The correct answer is A. Gravity diminishes when one is closer to the equator because the relative weight of the Earth is higher in this particular geographical location. See the last sentence of the passage, which explains how gravity becomes less robust, in other words weaker, as the distance from the equator diminishes.

15. The correct answer is E. Each leader was considered crucial due to his unique contribution. Each of these different reasons is stated in the passage: "Washington was chosen on the basis of being the first president. Jefferson was selected because he was instrumental in the writing of the American Declaration of Independence. Lincoln was selected on the basis of the mettle he demonstrated during the American Civil War and Roosevelt for his development of Square Deal policy, as well as being a proponent of the construction of the Panama Canal."

16. The correct answer is B. In the context of war, we can surmise that "mettle" means courage.

17. The correct answer is D. You need to add up the three points, represented by the diamond, square, and triangle on each line, for each contributor (Private, State, Federal, Charitable, and Other).

Here are the totals for the five contributors:

Private – 3,400

State – 3,800

Federal – 4,550

Charitable – 5,750

Other – 2,790

Therefore, the category of charitable is the highest.

18. The correct answer is E. The writer's primary persuasive technique is using statistical evidence. Examples of this can be seen in the phrases "30 times more likely" and "12% chance" in paragraph 2.

19. The correct answer is E. Sentence 8 states: "This outcome is inherently unfair because economic rewards should be judged by and distributed according to the worthiness of the employment to society as a whole, rather than according to social status or prestige." The words "unfair," "should," and "worthiness" in this sentence demonstrate that an opinion is being given.

20. The correct answer is D. Sentence 4 states: "Both boys have the same hobbies and musical tastes." The hobbies and tastes of the boys are not related to their academic performance, which is the subject of this passage.

21. The correct answer is C. The sentence before the gap states: "the previous buildings constructed on this site were limited by the soft and often water-logged ground in the surrounding area." The sentence after the gap is: "This assessment was necessary in order to ensure that subsidence, and potential collapse of the new structure, could be averted." The phrase "this assessment" in the last sentence relates to the idea of carefully assessing the water supply, which is mentioned in answer C, as well as in the sentence preceding the gap.

22. The correct answer is C. The statement that best represents the writer's opinion is that "Careful planning is paramount for construction projects in urban settings." Paragraph 2 of the passage talks about how careful planning was needed because of the groundwater problem. Be careful if you wanted to choose answer D. This is a fact from the passage, not an opinion.

23. The correct answer is B. Between paragraphs 1 and 2, the writer's approach shifts from interesting facts to potential problems. The interesting facts in paragraph 1 are the various contributions to the project from different countries. The potential problems in paragraph 2 relate to the groundwater issue.

24. The correct answer is A. The primary purpose of the passage is to compare two areas of an academic discipline. Sentence 1 states: "The study of philosophy usually deals with two key problem areas: human choice and human thought." So, we can see that the academic discipline of philosophy is mentioned in this sentence. This sentence also talks about the two areas of the discipline, which are human choice and human thought.

25. The correct answer is A. The following sentence does not fit with the logical flow of the paragraph: "A consideration of these problem areas is not an aspect of psychology or art." The text is about philosophy, not psychology or art.

26. The correct answer is E. Both of these sentences begin with a shift in thought. In the first sentence, we shift from the idea that Lincoln had financial problems to the idea that he might become successful as US President. In the other sentence, we shift from the idea that Lincoln was the underdog to the idea that he won the election. The phrases "in spite of" and "although" show the kind of concession that is provided when shifts in thought like these occur in a passage.

27. The correct answer is C. Answer C is the best because it is gives the general ideas of each paragraph. Paragraph 1 talks about Lincoln's biographical information, while paragraph 2 describes his campaign and election. The other answers give only specific ideas from each of the paragraphs.

28. The correct answer is B. "Garnered" means earned. Lincoln earned his support though public speaking. You may have been tempted to choose answer D. However, the word "achieved" generally does not imply as much effort as does the word "garnered."

29. The correct answer is C. The assumption that influenced the writer is that Lincoln was an unlikely presidential candidate. The passage explains how Lincoln's age and financial situation were against him. Be careful if you wanted to choose answer D. The passage does not indicate or imply how Lincoln is regarded today, although you might be tempted to conclude this from your own knowledge.

30. The correct answer is D. The sentence before the gap states: "Such a slump in the market, if not properly regulated, could bring about a computer-led stock market crash." The sentence after the gap states: "For this reason, regulations have been put in place by NASDAQ, AMEX, and FTSE." The word "crash" from the previous sentence ties into the idea of "collapse" in answer D. The word "regulations" in the final sentence relates to how to control the possibility of such a crash or collapse.

31. The correct answer is C. This sentence from the passage best expresses its central idea: "Nevertheless, because of the high level of automation now involved in buying and selling shares, computer-to-computer trading could result in a downturn in the stock market." The passage goes on to talk about the consequences of improper regulations, so answer C is the best. You may have wanted to choose answer A, but it is not the best answer because the passage talks about how the controls are ineffective.

32. The correct answer is A. A likely conclusion regarding computer-to-computer trading is that it is usually regarded as being safer now than it has been in the past. Trading is safer now because of the regulations mentioned in paragraph 2. Answer B is a wild guess. Answers C, D, and E are not mentioned or implied in the passage.

33. The correct answer is E. The most appropriate title for this passage is "The Basics of Healthy Nutrition." This relates back to the rhetorical question in paragraph 1: "What does healthy nutrition consist of?"

34. The correct answer is A. The audience is most likely to be adults listening to a radio program on nutrition. The passage has a conversational tone, beginning sentences with words like "so" and "well."

35. The correct answer is B. We know that the word "deleterious" has a negative connotation because the passage is talking about disease at this point, so "harmful" is the best synonym.

36. The correct answer is B. According to the passage, the primary reason why manufacturers of processed food use additives is to improve the appearance of the food. In the second sentence of paragraph 2, we see that additives "enhance the color of food."

37. The correct answer is D. The metallurgical composition of a coin is determined to be correct by the electricity that has passed through the magnet. Paragraph 3 states: "Electricity passes through the magnet, causing the coin to slow down in some cases. If the coin begins to slow down, its metallurgic composition has been deemed to be correct." That is

to say, the coin slows down because of the electricity that has passed through the magnet.

38. The correct answer is B. The last step in testing the coin is the determination of its metallurgic composition. This step is provided in the last sentence of paragraph 3: "If the coin begins to slow down, its metallurgic composition has been deemed to be correct." Be careful if you chose answer D. The deflector is not a step in the testing process, but rather an alternative outcome of the test.

39. The correct answer is D. If the reader wants to see if this textbook has made any reference to another book, he or she should look in the bibliography. A bibliography is a list of references to other materials.

40. The correct answer is D. Part 4 is most likely to discuss whether inter-planetary space travel will be undertaken in the future. This topic would be discussed in the chapter entitled "The Universe Beyond."

41. The correct answer is A. The mention of "nine scenes" in answer A relates to the phrase "the scenes" at the start of the next sentence.

42. The correct answer is C. Michelangelo dismissed his assistants because he believed that they were inept craftsmen. See the last sentence of paragraph 1, which states that "as work proceeded, the artist dismissed each of his assistants one by one, claiming that they lacked the competence necessary to do the task at hand."

43. The correct answer is D. The following sentence expresses an opinion of the author rather than a fact: "Yet, he went on to paint one of the most

beautiful works in art history." The adjectival phrase "the most beautiful" indicates that an opinion is being given.

44. The correct answer is E. The two tools which were used to place the stones into their final positions on the pyramid were made from wood. Paragraph 3 mentions wooden rods and wooden rockers.

45. The correct answer is C. Between paragraphs 1 and 2, the writer's approach shifts from background information to specific details. Paragraph 1 describes tools in general, while paragraph 2 names specific tools.

46. The correct answer is C. The writer's main purpose is to give an overview of some of the main implements that were used to construct the Giza pyramids. The main purpose of the passage is implied in the last sentence of the first paragraph: "it is notable that the Egyptians had only the most primitive, handmade tools to complete the massive project.

47. The correct answer is A. The assumption that has most influenced the writer is that it is incredible that the Egyptians were able to construct the pyramids using only hand-made tools. The assumption that the outcome was incredible is shown by the contrast between the words "primitive" and "massive" in the last sentence of paragraph 1.

48. The correct answer is E. The following sentence from the passage best expresses its central idea: "Sadly, she too had been conditioned to learn that such actions were useless." The idea of conditioning is also mentioned in paragraph 2, with respect to the baby learning that crying would not change anything.

49. The correct answer is B. The woman sees that there is no point in such actions, so "useless" is the best answer.

50. The correct answer is E. The word "resigned" is a synonym of the phrase "mute and hopeless" in the last sentence.

CBEST Practice Reading Test 3

Look at the extract from an index below to answer the two questions that follow.

1. Where can the reader look to see whether the book contains information on how a person should warm up before undertaking aerobic exercise?

    A. Pages 243–254

    B. Pages 255–263

    C. Pages 264–273

    D. Pages 274–286

    E. Pages 287–297

2. How is the section of the book on the history of exercise organized?

    A. alphabetically

    B. chronologically

    C. by importance

    D. by type of exercise

    E. from least to most strenuous

Read the passage below and answer the three questions that follow.

Scientists have been conducting genetic engineering experiments for years. Gene splicing, the process whereby a small part of the DNA of one organism is removed and inserted into the DNA chain of another organism, has produced results like the super tomato. In order to create the super tomato, the gene resistant to cold temperatures on the DNA chain of a particular type of cold-water fish was isolated, removed, and inserted into an ordinary tomato plant. This resulted in a new type of tomato plant that can thrive in cold weather conditions.

However, gene splicing has become controversial lately. As animal rights groups have come more into prominence socially and politically, and people are more and more aware of the suffering of animals, many people question whether using animals in this way is medically reasonable, indeed whether it is even ethical or moral.

3.   From this passage, it seems safe to conclude that
     A. the super tomato was the first case of gene splicing.
     B. the super tomato is only one example of gene splicing.
     C. DNA from tomatoes has also been inserted into certain types of fish.
     D. the interests of animal rights groups will soon fade from the public eye.
     E. most people object to gene splicing.

4.   Which of the following statements gives the best summary of the main points of the lecture?
     A. Genetic engineering has a recent scientific background.
     B. DNA is the essential part of every living cell.
     C. The process of genetic engineering involves gene splicing of part of the DNA chain.
     D. The super-tomato can grow in severely cold conditions.
     E. Although gene splicing is not new, there have been ethical and moral debates about it recently.

5. Which of the following best describes the pattern of organization of this passage?

A. problem and solution

B. explanation and examples

C. background and recent debates

D. step-by-step instructions

E. order of importance

Read the passage below and answer the four questions that follow.

[1]In 1804, Meriwether Lewis and William Clark began an expedition across the western United States. [2]This area was then known as the Louisiana Territory. [3]The two men had met years earlier and established a long-lasting friendship. [4]At that time, Lewis was well-known as possessing an outgoing and amiable personality. [5]When Lewis was later a young captain in the army, he received a letter from President Thomas Jefferson offering him funding to explore the Western country.

[6]With Jefferson's permission, Lewis offered a partnership in the expedition to his trusted friend Clark. [7]When their journey had safely concluded 8,000 miles later, President Jefferson purchased the Louisiana Territory for fifteen million dollars. [8]Thus, the most important land acquisition in the history of the United States took place.

6. Which numbered sentence provides an opinion rather than a fact?

A. Sentence 3

B. Sentence 4

C. Sentence 6

D. Sentence 7

E. Sentence 8

7. Which numbered sentence is least relevant to the main idea of the first paragraph?

A. Sentence 1

B. Sentence 2

C. Sentence 3

D. Sentence 4

E. Sentence 5

8. The main purpose of the passage is:

A. to give the background to Lewis and Clark's westward expedition.

B. to defend the purchase of the Louisiana Territory.

C. to state a crucial decision made by Thomas Jefferson.

D. to provide biographical information on Lewis and Clark.

E. to compare the skills of Lewis and Clark.

9. Why did Clark travel with Lewis?

A. Lewis needed someone to do menial jobs.

B. Clark felt he needed a partner.

C. Because of financial restrictions.

D. Because they were good friends.

E. Because President Jefferson requested it.

Read the passage below and answer the three questions that follow.

The Watergate burglary had many aspects, but at its center was President Richard Nixon. _____ the investigation of the burglary, government officials denied involvement in the crime. An extensive cover-up operation followed in an attempt to conceal those who were involved in planning the break-in. Yet, this <u>subterfuge</u> failed when the FBI investigated the one-hundred-dollar bills that were found in the pockets of the burglars. After making inquiries, the FBI discovered that this money originated from the Committee for the Re-election of the President, thereby confirming governmental involvement. _____ , individuals who had entered the highest branches of the American government to serve and protect the people went to prison instead.

10. Which of the words or phrases, if inserted in order into the blanks of the passage, would help the reader better understand the sequence of events?
    A. However; Yet
    B. Although; As a result
    C. While; Finally
    D. During; However
    E. Throughout; In the end

11. What is the main reason why the cover-up of the Watergate break-in failed?
    A. because the Committee for the Re-election of the President denied involvement
    B. because of the subterfuge of the FBI

C. because the burglars' money was traced back to a governmental organization

D. because its ringleaders went to prison

E. because of the number of governmental officials in high-level positions

12. Which of the following is the best meaning of the word <u>subterfuge</u> as it is used in this passage?

A. discovery

B. concealment

C. dishonesty

D. investigation

E. crime

Read the passage below and answer the three questions that follow.

Our ability to measure brain activity is owing to the research of two European scientists. It was in 1929 that electrical activity in the human brain was first discovered. Hans Berger, the German psychiatrist who made the discovery, was despondent to find out, however, that many other scientists quickly dismissed his research. The work of Berger was confirmed three years later when Edgar Adrian, a Briton, clearly demonstrated that the brain, like the heart, is profuse in its electrical activity. Because of Adrian's work, we know that the electrical impulses in the brain are a mixture of four different frequencies. _____

_____ .

These four frequencies are called alpha, beta, delta, and theta.

13. Which sentence, if inserted into the blank line in the paragraph, would best fit into the logical development of the passage?

    A. By "frequency," we are referring to the number of electrical impulses that occur in the brain per second.

    B. Improper sleep patterns can cause brain frequencies to become irregular.

    C. Because of the stress of modern life, many people today suffer from interruptions to the natural electrical activity in their brains.

    D. Adrian was often called "the mad genius" by his contemporaries.

    E. Adrian's work soon began to outshine that of Berger.

14. The information the writer conveys in this passage is addressed mainly to:

    A. doctors attending a professional seminar.

    B. practicing brain surgeons.

    C. a television documentary on brain research.

    D. the general public.

    E. elementary schoolchildren.

15. What is the writer's opinion regarding the work of Hans Berger?

    A. It was proper that his work was dismissed by the scientific community.

    B. Berger's work was inferior to that of Adrian.

    C. Berger's work paved the way for the research of Adrian.

D. Berger should have been more self-promoting about his discovery.

E. Berger's work was one of the most important discoveries of the 20th century.

Read the passage below and answer the three questions that follow.

The most significant characteristic of any population is its age-sex structure, defined as the proportion of people of each gender in various age groups. The age-sex structure determines the potential for reproduction, and therefore population growth. Thus, the age-sex structure has social policy implications. For instance, a population with a high proportion of elderly citizens needs to consider its governmentally-funded pension schemes and health care systems. Conversely, a greater percentage of young children in the population might imply that educational funding and child welfare policies need to be evaluated. Accordingly, as the composition of a population changes over time, the government may need to re-evaluate its funding priorities.

16. Governmental funding decisions should primarily be based on:
     A. the composition of the age-sex groups within its population.
     B. the number of elderly citizens in its population.
     C. the percentage of children in its population.
     D. reproduction rates.
     E. social policy limitations.

17. What is the writer's primary persuasive technique?

    A. giving emotional pleas

    B. citing known authorities

    C. predicting opposing viewpoints

    D. listing priorities in order of importance

    E. using compelling examples

18. Which of the following assumptions has most greatly influenced the writer?

    A. Health care systems are one of the most important needs of society.

    B. The government needs to do more in order to support senior citizens.

    C. The number of young children in the population has risen at an alarming rate.

    D. Society needs to consider the requirements of all of its members and balance competing needs carefully.

    E. The conflicting interests of various social groups put an unnecessary strain on the government.

Use the graph below to answer the question that follows.

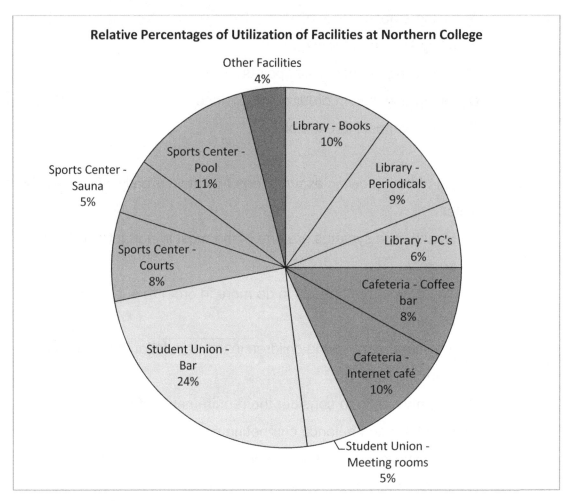

Relative Percentages of Utilization of Facilities at Northern College

Other Facilities 4%

Library - Books 10%

Library - Periodicals 9%

Sports Center - Pool 11%

Sports Center - Sauna 5%

Library - PC's 6%

Sports Center - Courts 8%

Cafeteria - Coffee bar 8%

Student Union - Bar 24%

Cafeteria - Internet café 10%

Student Union - Meeting rooms 5%

19. According to the graph, which area of the university has the highest percentage of use in total?

   A. Library

   B. Cafeteria

   C. Student Union

   D. Sports Center

   E. Other Facilities

Read the passage below and answer the three questions that follow.

I. In 1749, British surveyors spotted a high peak in the distant range of the Himalayas. More than 100 years later, in 1852, another survey was completed, which confirmed that this peak was the highest mountain in the world. Later named Mount Everest, this peak was unquestionably considered to be the world's highest mountain.

II. However, in 1986 George Wallerstein from the University of Washington posited that another Himalayan mountain, named K-2, was higher than Everest. It took an expedition of Italian scientists, who used a surfeit of technological devices, to disprove Wallerstein's claim.

20.   What is the nearest synonym to the word surfeit in the passage?
      A. enhancement
      B. plethora
      C. collection
      D. survey
      E. variety

21.   Which of the following groups of statements best summarizes the main topics addressed in each paragraph?
      A. I. Himalayan mountain expeditions; II. Research of Italian scientists
      B. I. The discovery of Mount Everest; II. University of Washington research
      C. I. Expeditions and discoveries in the Himalayas; II. Proving Wallerstein's claim

D. **I.** British explorers in the Himalayas; **II.** Wallerstein's research

E. **I.** Discovery and survey of Mount Everest; **II.** Confirmation of Everest's status

22. According to the passage, which one of the following statements is correct?

A. Since 1749, Mount Everest has universally been considered to be the tallest mountain in the world.

B. Wallerstein fell into disrepute in the academic community after his claims were disproved.

C. The University of Washington fully supported Wallerstien's claims about K-2.

D. The Italian team confirmed that Everest was, in fact, the tallest mountain in the world.

E. In spite of a lack of technologically-advanced equipment, Italian scientists were able to refute Wallerstein's hypothesis.

Read the passage below and answer the four questions that follow.

Owing to the powerful and destructive nature of tornadoes, there are, perhaps not surprisingly, a number of myths and misconceptions surrounding them. _____

_____ . Yet, <u>waterspouts</u>, tornadoes that form over bodies of water, often move onshore and cause extensive damage to coastal areas. In addition, tornadoes can accompany hurricanes and tropical storms as they move to land. Another common myth about tornadoes is that damage to built structures, like houses and office buildings, can be avoided if windows are opened prior to the impact of the storm.

Drivers often attempt to outrun tornadoes in their cars, but it is extremely unsafe to do so. Automobiles offer very little protection when twisters strike, so drivers should abandon their vehicles and seek safe shelter. Mobile homes are extremely vulnerable, so residents of these homes should go to the underground floor of the sturdiest nearby building. In the case of a building having no underground area, a person should go to the lowest floor of the building and place him or herself under a piece of heavy furniture.

23. What inference about the public's knowledge of tornadoes can be drawn from the passage?

    A. A large number of people know how to avoid tornado damage.

    B. Most people appreciate the risk of death associated with tornadoes.

    C. Some members of the public know how to regulate the pressure inside buildings.

    D. Many people are not fully aware of certain key information about tornadoes.

    E. Many members of the public have an irrational fear of tornadoes.

24. Based on the information contained in the passage, which of the following best explains the term <u>waterspouts</u> in paragraph 1?

    A. Tornadoes that move away from coastal areas

    B. Tornadoes that occur over oceans, rivers, and lakes

C. Tornadoes that occur onshore

D. Tornadoes that accompany tropical storms and hurricanes

E. Tornadoes that damage built structures

25. Which sentence if placed in the line in paragraph 1 would be the most consistent with the writer's purpose and audience?

A. Indeed, the highest number of deaths and injuries are not caused by the winds themselves, but by flying objects and other debris.

B. For instance, many people mistakenly believe that tornadoes never occur over rivers, lakes, and oceans.

C. Therefore, public safety is of the utmost importance when a tornado strikes.

D. For this reason, local governments must act quickly to put early severe weather warning systems into place.

E. Tornadoes are often far different than those depicted in action movies.

26. According to the passage, what is the safest place to be when a tornado strikes?

A. an abandoned vehicle

B. mobile homes

C. the basement of a building

D. under a piece of sturdy furniture

E. under a bridge

Read the passage below and answer the two questions that follow.

Jean Piaget was the most influential thinker in the area of child development in the twentieth century. Due to his training as a biologist, Piaget theorized that children go through a stage of assimilation as they grow to maturity. Assimilation refers to the process of transforming one's environment in order to bring about its conformance to innate or inborn cognitive processes. For instance, schemes used in infant breast feeding and bottle feeding are examples of assimilation. That is because the child utilizes his or her innate capacity for sucking to complete both tasks.

27.   Which of the following sentences from the passage expresses an opinion rather than a fact?

   A. Jean Piaget was the most influential thinker in the area of child development in the twentieth century.

   B. Due to his training as a biologist, Piaget theorized that children go through a stage of assimilation as they grow to maturity.

   C. Assimilation refers to the process of transforming one's environment in order to bring about its conformance to innate or inborn cognitive processes.

   D. For instance, schemes used in infant breast feeding and bottle feeding are examples of assimilation.

   E. That is because the child utilizes his or her innate capacity for sucking to complete both tasks.

28.   Which sentence from the passage best expresses its central idea?

   A. Jean Piaget was the most influential thinker in the area of child development in the twentieth century.

   B. Due to his training as a biologist, Piaget theorized that children go through a stage of assimilation as they grow to maturity.

   C. Assimilation refers to the process of transforming one's environment in order to bring about its conformance to innate or inborn cognitive processes.

   D. For instance, schemes used in infant breast feeding and bottle feeding are examples of assimilation.

   E. That is because the child utilizes his or her innate capacity for sucking to complete both tasks.

Read the passage below and answer the two questions that follow.

Inherent social and cultural biases pervaded the manner in which archeological findings were investigated during the early nineteenth century because little attention was paid to the roles that wealth, status, and nationality played in the recovery and interpretation of the artifacts. _____ , in the 1860s Charles Darwin established the theory that human beings are the ultimate product of a long biological evolutionary process. Darwinian theory infiltrated the discipline of archeology and heavily influenced the manner in which archeological artifacts are now recovered and analyzed. _____ Darwinism, there has been a surge in artifacts excavated from Africa and Asia.

29. Which of the words or phrases, if inserted in order into the blanks of the passage, would help the reader better understand the sequence of events?

A. Then; As a result of

B. Although; In spite of

C. While; Finally

D. During; However

E. Yet; In the end

30. Based on the information contained in the passage, what is a likely conclusion regarding archeological methods?

A. They need to remain static to be useful.

B. They should create cultural differences.

C. They have developed a good deal when compared to earlier centuries.

D. They should not have been rectified in countries in the Far East.

E. They must be based on Darwinian theory in order to be valid.

Read the passage below and answer the three questions that follow.

The ancient Egyptians used eye shadow over 5,000 years ago. The cosmetic was used for personal beautification, as well as for practical reasons. Consisting of a paste made from malachite, a copper salt that was bright green, the eye paint protected against glare from the sun, in addition to being an attractive color. On her upper eye lids, Cleopatra wore blue eye shadow made of ground lapis lazuli stone, much like other women of her day.

The queen used green malachite as an accent below her eyes, and kohl, which consisted of lead sulfide, to provide color to her eyelashes and eyebrows. Red ochre, iron-based clay, provided her with lip and cheek color. Henna, a reddish-brown dye that was derived from a bush, was also commonly used by women in those days as a nail polish. _____ _____ . The use of this particular cosmetic was not limited to women. Men also used the substance to darken their hair and beards.

31. Which sentence, if inserted into the blank in paragraph 2, would be the most consistent with the author's purpose?

    A. Extracts from the henna bush could also be used for medicinal purposes.

    B. The henna was thickened with tannin from the bark or fruit of various trees in order to be suitable for cosmetic use.

    C. Henna is also used nowadays for decoration of the hands and feet.

D. Certain environmental activists are concerned about the use of henna in this way.

E. The henna plant has often been the subject of botanical investigations.

32. Which of the following outlines best describes the organization of the topics addressed in paragraphs I and II?

A. I. Cosmetic uses of malachite; II. The beautification of Cleopatra

B. I. Cosmetics in ancient Egypt; II. Cosmetic uses of henna

C. I. The ancient Egyptians; II. The use of minerals in cosmetics

D. I. Ancient Egyptian eye shadow; II. Other ancient cosmetics

E. I. The history of personal beautification; II. Uses of cosmetics by men

33. What word best describes the style of writing in this passage?

A. argumentative

B. persuasive

C. informative

D. condemning

E. balanced

Read the passage below and answer the three questions that follow.

Acid has been present in rain for millennia, naturally occurring from volcanoes and plankton. However, scientific research shows that the acid content of rain has increased dramatically over the past two hundred years, in spite of humanity's recent attempts to control the problem.

Rain consists of two elements, nitrogen and sulfur. When sulfur is burned, it transforms into sulfur dioxide. Nitrogen also oxides when burned. When released from factories into the atmosphere, both sulfur dioxide and nitrogen oxide react with the water molecules in rain to form sulfuric acid and nitric acid, respectively.

Factories and other enterprises have built high chimneys in an attempt to carry these gases away from urban areas. Nevertheless, the effect of the structures has been to spread the gases more thinly and widely in the atmosphere, thereby exacerbating the problem.

The acid in rain also emanates from automobile exhaust, domestic residences, and power stations. <u>The latter have been the culprit of the bulk</u> of the acid in rainwater in recent years. Since the pollutants are carried by the wind, countries can experience acid rain from pollution that was generated in countries thousands of miles away.

34.   Which one of the following phrases is closest in meaning to <u>the latter have been the culprit of the bulk</u> as it is used in the above text?

   A. Automobile exhaust has caused the majority of acid rain.

B. Automobile exhaust, domestic residences, and power stations have equally contributed to the creation of acid rain.

C. Power stations are more widespread geographically than other causes of acid rain.

D. Power stations generate a great deal of pollution that is carried by the wind.

E. Power stations have been the largest contributor to the problem.

35. Between paragraphs 2 and 3, the writer's approach shifts from:

A. scientific explanation to current problems

B. chemical analysis to scientific inquiry

C. historical background to current problems

D. scientific inquiry to possible solutions

E. cause to effect

36. Which detail from the passage best supports the writer's main idea?

A. When sulfur is burned, it transforms into sulfur dioxide.

B. When released from factories into the atmosphere, both sulfur dioxide and nitrogen oxide react with the water molecules in rain to form sulfuric acid and nitric acid, respectively.

C. Nevertheless, the effect of the structures has been to spread the gases more thinly and widely in the atmosphere, thereby exacerbating the problem.

D. The acid in rain also emanates from automobile exhaust, domestic residences, and power stations.

E. Since the pollutants are carried by the wind, countries can experience acid rain from pollution that was generated in countries thousands of miles away.

Read the passage below and answer the two questions that follow.

The tradition of music in the western world originated in the genre of chanting. Chant, a monophonic form of music, was the dominant mode of music prior to the thirteenth century. The semantic origins of the word "monophonic" are interesting to etymologists. "Mono" is from a Greek word which means one thing alone or by itself. "Phonic" is also Greek in origin, and it means sound. Accordingly, monophonic music consists of only one sound or voice that combines various notes in a series. Polyphonic music appeared during the early Renaissance period. In contrast to monophonic music, polyphonic music consists of more than one voice or instrument, and it combines the notes from the different sources together simultaneously.

37.   Which sentence is least relevant to the main idea of the passage?

A. The tradition of music in the western world originated in the genre of chanting.

B. Chant, a monophonic form of music, was the dominant mode of music prior to the thirteenth century.

C. The semantic origins of the word "monophonic" are interesting to etymologists.

D. "Mono" is from a Greek word which means one thing alone or by itself.

E. Polyphonic music appeared during the early Renaissance period.

38. Who is this passage most likely addressed to?

A. the general public

B. a college class on music theory

C. a student during a music lesson

D. a group of classical composers

E. elementary age children

Look at the table of contents below from a horticultural textbook in order to answer the two questions that follow.

39. Which part of the book is likely to contain information on why the leaves of certain trees change color in the autumn?
   A. Introduction
   B. Chapter One
   C. Chapter Two
   D. Chapter Three
   E. Chapter Four

40. A reader wants to find the definition of the phrase "environmental runoff." Where can the reader find this information the most quickly?
   A. Introduction
   B. Chapter One
   C. Glossary
   D. Bibliography
   E. Index

Read the passage below and answer the two questions that follow.

Baking a cake is easy, provided you have a good oven and the correct ingredients. For a moist and fluffy cake, you should first of all pre-heat the oven to 350 degrees Fahrenheit. Be absolutely sure that the oven is pre-heated to the correct temperature. While the oven is pre-heating, you can grease and flour your cake pan and mix your ingredients together.

Before adding the wet ingredients, mix the dry ingredients together. The latter consist of one and a half cups of sugar, one teaspoon of salt, two teaspoons of baking soda, and two cups of sifted flour, which should be mixed well in a large bowl. However, before proceeding with the mixture, ensure that the bowl is of a sufficient size to accommodate all of the ingredients. Now add one-half cup of vegetable shortening, two eggs, one cup of whole milk, and a teaspoon of vanilla.

Put the mixture into the cake pan, bake for 30 minutes, and enjoy!

41. Based on the instructions above, it is likely that failing to pre-heat the oven will result in:
     A. damage to the oven.
     B. the cake being burnt.
     C. the cake taking longer to bake.
     D. insufficient time to prepare the cake pan.
     E. the cake being dry and dense.

42. What should one do after preparing the cake pan?
     A. add the wet ingredients
     B. check that the mixing bowl is large enough
     C. mix the sugar, salt, baking soda, and flour together
     D. check the oven temperature
     E. add the shortening, eggs, milk, and vanilla

Read the passage below and answer the four questions that follow.

An efficient electron microscope can magnify an object by more than one million times its original size. This innovation has thereby allowed scientists to study the precise molecules that constitute human life.

The electron microscope functions by emitting a stream of electrons from a gun-type instrument, which is similar to the <u>apparatus</u> used in an old-fashioned television tube. The electrons pass through an advanced electronic field that is accelerated to millions of volts in certain cases. Before traveling through a vacuum in order to remove oxygen molecules, the electrons are focused into a beam by way of magnetic coils.

Invisible to the naked eye, electron beams can nevertheless be projected onto a florescent screen. When striking the screen, the electrons glow and can even be recorded on film. Cameras also use film to capture images.

In the transmission electron microscope, which is used to study cells or tissues, the beam passes through a thin slice of the specimen that is being studied. On the other hand, in the scanning electron microscope, which is used for tasks such as examining bullets and fibers, the beam is reflected. This reflection creates a picture of the specimen line by line.

43.   What is the last step in the process by which the beam emanating from the electron microscope is formed?

   A. The electrons pass through an electronic field.

   B. The electrons are accelerated to millions of volts.

   C. The electrons travel through a vacuum.

   D. Oxygen is removed from the molecules.

   E. The electrons pass through magnetic coils.

44. What is the closest synonym to the word <u>apparatus</u> as it is used in the passage?

A. machine

B. electricity

C. device

D. tube

E. bulb

45. Which of the following assumptions has influenced the writer?

A. The electron microscope has proven to be an extremely important invention for the scientific community.

B. The invention of the electron microscope would have been impossible without the prior invention of the television.

C. The electron microscope cannot function without projection onto a florescent screen.

D. The transmission electron microscope is inferior to the scanning electron microscope.

E. The electron microscope will soon be an outdated technology.

46. Which statement does not fit the logical flow of the text?

A. This innovation has thereby allowed scientists to study the precise molecules that constitute human life.

B. The electrons pass through an advanced electronic field that is accelerated to millions of volts in certain cases.

C. When striking the screen, the electrons glow and can even be recorded on film.

D. Cameras also use film to capture images.

E. This reflection creates a picture of the specimen line by line.

Read the passage below and answer the four questions that follow.

Oliver, having taken down the shutters, was graciously assisted by Noah, who having consoled him with the assurance that "he'd catch it," condescended to help him. Mr. Snowberry came down soon after.

Shortly afterwards, Mrs. Snowberry appeared. Oliver having "caught it," in fulfillment of Noah's prediction, followed the young gentleman down the stairs to breakfast.

"Come near the fire, Noah," said Charlotte. "I have saved a nice little bit of bacon for you from master's breakfast."

"Do you hear?" said Noah.

"Lord, Noah!" said Charlotte.

"Let him alone!" said Noah. "Why everybody lets him alone enough, for the matter of that."

"Oh, you queer soul!" said Charlotte, bursting into a hearty laugh. She was then joined by Noah, after which they both looked scornfully at poor Oliver Twist.

Noah was a charity boy, but not a workhouse orphan. He could trace his genealogy back to his parents, who lived hard by; his mother being a washerwoman, and his father a drunken soldier, discharged with a wooden leg, and a diurnal pension of twopence-halfpenny and an unstable fraction. The shop boys in the neighborhood had long been in the habit of branding Noah, in the public streets, with the ignominious epithets of "leathers," "charity," and the like; and Noah had borne them without reply. But now that fortune had cast his way a nameless orphan, at whom even the meanest could point the finger of scorn, he retorted on him with interest.

Adapted from *Oliver Twist* by Charles Dickens

47. What is the meaning of "he'd catch it" in the first paragraph of the passage?
   A. he'd find it
   B. he'd buy it
   C. he'd be saved
   D. he would be laughed at
   E. he would be punished

48. According to the passage, Oliver could be described as:
   A. gracious
   B. scornful
   C. ignominious
   D. esteemed
   E. ridiculed

49. The passage mainly illustrates:
   A. Charlotte's contempt of orphans.
   B. the wealth of the Snowberry family.
   C. the exploits of Oliver Twist.
   D. Noah's childhood experiences.
   E. the relationship between Noah and Oliver.

50. Who is the "nameless orphan" mentioned in the passage?

A. charity boys

B. workhouse orphans

C. Noah

D. Oliver

E. Charlotte

ANSWER KEY AND EXPLANATIONS

Practice Reading Test 3

1. The correct answer is A. You will find the answer in the second item in the index "Exercise: aerobic 243–254." Be careful if you chose answer D. Pages 274–286 are talking about the dangers of exercise in general, not about aerobic exercise in particular.

2. The correct answer is B. You will find the answer in the part of the index on "Exercise: history of 238–242." You can see here that the entries in this section of the index are in chronological order from the 17th century to the 21st century.

3. The correct answer is B. The passage states that gene splicing "has produced results like the super tomato." The phrase "results like" indicates that the super tomato is just one example of this phenomenon.

4. The correct answer is E. Paragraph 1 provides background information on gene splicing, while paragraph 2 gives a brief overview of the ethical and moral debates relating to the topic.

5. The correct answer is C. Please notice the phrase "controversial lately" in the first sentence of paragraph 2, which indicates that there are recent debates about this topic, so the pattern of organization of the passage is "background and recent debates."

6. The correct answer is E. Sentence number 8 contains an opinion when it uses the adjectival phrase "the most important." Answer A is not correct

because there would have been historical evidence to show that the friendship between Lewis and Clark existed. Answer B is not correct because this was, in fact, how Lewis was known.

7. The correct answer is D. Sentence 4 comments that Lewis's personality was outgoing and amiable. This is a personal detail which is unrelated to the historical facts in the passage.

8. The correct answer is A. The passage begins with the date of the start of the expedition and talks about the facts that made the expedition possible, so it is giving background information.

9. The correct answer is D. This answer is supported by sentences 3 and 6, which state that Clark was Lewis's trusted friend.

10. The correct answer is E. "Throughout" is the best answer for the first gap because the investigation spanned a certain period of time. "In the end" is the best answer for the second gap because it is to be placed at the beginning of the last sentence of the passage.

11. The correct answer is C. The second to the last sentence of the passage states: "After making inquiries, the FBI discovered that this money originated from the Committee for the Re-election of the President, thereby confirming governmental involvement." Therefore, we can conclude that the Watergate break-in failed because the burglars' money was traced back to a governmental organization, namely the Committee for the Re-election of the President.

12. The correct answer is B. For these types of questions, you need to look for synonyms in the passage. In this passage, "cover-up" is a synonym for "subterfuge," which means concealment.

13. The correct answer is A. This sentence is the best one because the sentences before and after it mention frequencies, so the definition of the word "frequency" is appropriate here.

14. The correct answer is C. The level of vocabulary and technical information in the passage indicate that it is an informative program about brain research. The passage is not technical enough for doctors or surgeons, but it contains too much detail for the general public or for school children.

15. The correct answer is C. The fourth sentence of the passage states: "The work of Berger was confirmed three years later when Edgar Adrian, a Briton, clearly demonstrated that the brain, like the heart, is profuse in its electrical activity." In other words, Adrian confirmed Berger's findings, so Berger paved the way or established a starting point for Adrian.

16. The correct answer is A. The passage implies that governmental funding decisions should primarily be based on the composition of the age-sex groups within its population. This answer is supported by the first sentence in the passage, which states that the age-sex structure is the most significant characteristic of any population.

17. The correct answer is E. The writer gives the examples of elderly citizens and young children in the passage.

18. The correct answer is D. The writer has assumed that society, by way of the government, needs to consider the requirements of all of its members and balance competing needs carefully. This assumption is implied in the last sentence of the passage, which states that "as the composition of a population changes over time, the government may need to re-evaluate its funding priorities."

19. The correct answer is C. Read the graph carefully, do the math, and then check your answers for questions like this one. The library equals 25%, the cafeteria is 18%, the student union is 29%, the sports center is 24%, and other facilities total 4%, so the student union is the highest.

20. The correct answer is B. The passage states: "It took an expedition of Italian scientists, who used a surfeit of technological devices, to disprove Wallerstein's claim." "Plethora," from answer B, means a huge quantity of something. In the passage, a mammoth effort is implied by the phrase "It took an expedition of Italian scientists."

21. The correct answer is E. Paragraph 1 gives the background to the discovery and survey of the peak named Mount Everest, and paragraph 2 talks about disproving Wallerstein's claim, which confirmed the status of Mount Everest as the highest peak in the world. Therefore, "Discovery and survey of Mount Everest" is the best summary of paragraph 1, while "Confirmation of Everest's status" is the best summary of paragraph 2.

22. The correct answer is D. The Italian team confirmed that Everest was, in fact, the tallest mountain in the world. This answer is supported by the last sentence in the passage, which states: "It took an expedition of Italian

scientists, who used a surfeit of technological devices, to disprove Wallerstein's claim."

23. The correct answer is D. Many people are not fully aware of certain key information about tornadoes. This lack of awareness is implied by the phrase "myths and misconceptions" in the first sentence of the first paragraph.

24. The correct answer is B. Waterspouts are tornadoes that occur over oceans, rivers, and lakes. See the phrase "bodies of water" in sentence 3 of paragraph 1.

25. The correct answer is B. The phrase "rivers, lakes, and oceans" in answer B ties into the idea of "bodies of water," which is mentioned in the next sentence in the passage.

26. The correct answer is C. Sentence 3 in paragraph 2 gives the recommendation of going to "the underground floor," which means the basement.

27. The correct answer is A. The adjectival phrase "the most influential" in the first sentence indicates that an opinion is being given.

28. The correct answer is B. Answer B is the most general one, and is therefore the best choice. Answer A gives background information, not the central idea. Answer C provides a definition, answer D gives an example, and answer E gives an explanation.

29. The correct answer is A. "Then" is the most suitable for the first gap because the events are being given in chronological order. "As a result" is the best for the last sentence because a conclusion is being stated.

30. The correct answer is C. The last sentence of the passage states that "there has been a surge in artifacts excavated from Africa and Asia." The phrase "has been a surge" indicates that a good deal of development has occurred when compared to earlier centuries.

31. The correct answer is B. The cosmetic use of henna is mentioned in the previous sentence. The phrase "this particular cosmetic" in the sentence after the gap also refers to the cosmetic use of henna.

32. The correct answer is D. Paragraph 1 is devoted exclusively to the topic of eye shadow, while paragraph 2 talks about eye liner, lip and cheek color, nail polish, and hair dye, so the best summaries are "Ancient Egyptian eye shadow" for the first paragraph and "Other ancient cosmetics" for the second paragraph.

33. The correct answer is C. The passage focuses on historical facts, such as Cleopatra's use of cosmetics and the history of the cosmetic use of henna. Thus, the passage is informative in nature.

34. The correct answer is E. The second sentence of the last paragraph mentions that power stations "have been the culprit of the bulk of the acid in rainwater in recent years," meaning that they are the largest contributor to the problem.

35. The correct answer is A. The mention of the chemicals nitrogen and sulfur in paragraph 2 shows that a scientific explanation is being provided. Paragraph 3 talks about "exacerbating the problem," indicating that current problems are being discussed. Accordingly, the writer's approach shifts from scientific explanation to current problems.

36. The correct answer is C. The statement that best supports the writer's main idea is that "the effect of the structures has been to spread the gases more thinly and widely in the atmosphere, thereby exacerbating the problem." This statement links back to the main idea of the passage, which is stated in paragraph 1, sentence 2: "scientific research shows that the acid content of rain has increased dramatically over the past two hundred years, in spite of humanity's recent attempts to control the problem."

37. The correct answer is C. The passage is about music, rather than linguistics, so the sentence stating that "the semantic origins of the word 'monophonic' are interesting to etymologists" is somewhat out of place.

38. The correct answer is B. The academic vocabulary, such as the words "monophonic" and "polyphonic," indicates that the talk is aimed at college students studying music theory. The talk is too formal for an individual music lesson.

39. The correct answer is D. Deciduous trees are those whose leaves change color in the autumn, so chapter 3 will discuss this phenomenon.

40. The correct answer is C. A glossary is the part of a book that provides definitions.

41. The correct answer is E. Sentence 2 mentions what needs to be done to have a moist and fluffy cake. If this advice is not followed, one will get the opposite result, a cake that is dry and dense.

42. The correct answer is B. Be careful when answering questions like this one because the sentences in the passage may not be given in the correct order. Notice the sentence "However, before proceeding with the mixture, ensure that the bowl is of a sufficient size," which indicates that you must check the size of the bowl after preparing the pan and before mixing the ingredients.

43. The correct answer is E. The last step in the process for forming the beam is that the electrons pass through magnetic coils. This answer is found in the last sentence of paragraph 2, which states: "Before traveling through a vacuum in order to remove oxygen molecules, the electrons are focused into a beam by way of magnetic coils." Note that the question focuses on the process of forming the beam in particular, not on the movement of electrons in general, so answer C is incorrect.

44. The correct answer is C. The passage compares the microscope to a television tube in the first sentence of paragraph 2. Both of these items are electronic devices. Machines are larger than devices, so answer A is not the best answer.

45. The correct answer is A. The assumption that has influenced the writer is that the electron microscope has proven to be an extremely important invention for the scientific community. This answer is supported by the second sentence of paragraph 1: "This innovation [i.e., the electron

microscope] has thereby allowed scientists to study the precise molecules that constitute human life."

46. The correct answer is D. The statement that "cameras also use film to capture images" does not fit the logical flow of the text. Nothing else about cameras is mentioned in the passage.

47. The correct answer is E. "He'd catch it" means that Oliver was to be punished. This interpretation is supported by paragraph 2, which implies that Mrs. Snowberry is an authoritarian whom the boys fear.

48. The correct answer is E. Noah exclaims about Oliver: "Let him alone!" This exclamation indicates that Oliver is the source of ridicule. The passage also mentions that Oliver is scorned, which is synonymous with being ridiculed.

49. The correct answer is E. The passage mainly illustrates the relationship between Noah and Oliver. This idea is illustrated especially clearly in the last paragraph of the passage, in which we see Noah's view of Oliver.

50. The correct answer is D. The last sentence of the passage states: "But now that fortune had cast his way a nameless orphan, at whom even the meanest could point the finger of scorn, he retorted on him with interest." In this sentence, "his" refers to Noah, so the "nameless orphan" must refer to Oliver.

CBEST Practice Reading Test 4

Read the passage below and answer the three questions that follow.

Equating the whole history of the struggle of humankind to that of the class struggle, the social and political writings of Karl Marx have been the impetus of a great deal of change within society. According to Marxism, the political school of thought based on Marx's doctrines, the working class should strive to defeat capitalism, since capitalistic societies inherently have within them a dynamic that results in the wealthy ruling classes oppressing the masses. The nation state is seen as an instrument of class rule because it supports private capital and suppresses the common person through economic mechanisms, such as the taxation of wages. Because growth of private capital is stimulated by earning profits and extracting surplus value in the production process, wages have to be kept low.

Since capitalism reduces the purchasing power of workers to consume the goods that they produce, Marx emphasized that capitalism inheres in a central contradiction. Under the tenets of Marxism, capitalism is therefore inherently unstable. Marx asserted that productive power ideally should be in the hands of the general public, which would cause class differences to vanish. These idealistic writings have had a huge impact on culture and politics; yet, many believe that Marx's work lacked the practical details needed to bring about the changes to the class structure that he envisaged.

1.   The primary purpose of the first paragraph is to:

A. discuss why the writings of Karl Marx have had such enduring social and political importance.

B. explain the basic tenets of Marxism, before going on to discuss Marxist views on capitalism and the consequences of private capital.

C. critique the existing class structure and oppression of the masses.

D. decry the manner in which taxation and earning profits cause wages to be lowered.

E. recount the cultural and historical significance of the work of Karl Marx.

2.   Which of the following groups of statements best summarizes the main topics addressed in each paragraph?

A. I. The first paragraph states an assertion; II. The second paragraph refutes that assertion with statistical evidence.

B. I. The first paragraph explains a long-standing problem; II. The second paragraph provides the potential solution.

C. I. The first paragraph introduces and expounds upon a theory; II. The second paragraph points out criticisms of the theory.

D. I. The first paragraph gives the background to the topic in a general way; II. The second paragraph provides specific details about the topic.

E. I. The first paragraph describes a phenomenon; II. The second paragraph provides further examples of the phenomenon.

3. The writer mentions the "huge impact" that these writings have had on culture and politics in the last sentence in order to:

   A. underscore the fact that class differences have not yet vanished.

   B. highlight the way in which capitalism is often unstable.

   C. reiterate the importance of giving power back to the general populace.

   D. lament the social change that Marx himself predicted.

   E. juxtapose this impact to Marx's failure to include pragmatic instructions in his work.

Read the passage below and answer the three questions that follow.

[1]Recent research shows that social media platforms may actually be making us antisocial. [2]Survey results indicate that many people would prefer to interact on Facebook or Twitter, rather than see friends and family in person. [3]The primary reason cited for this phenomenon was that one does not need to go to the effort to dress up and travel in order to use these social media platforms.

[4]Another independent survey revealed that people often remain glued to their hand-held devices to check their social media when they do go out with friends. [5]Therefore, social media platforms are definitely having a detrimental impact upon our social skills and interpersonal relationships.

4. In the second paragraph, the author implies that the effect of social media on relationships has largely been:

A. deleterious

B. ambivalent

C. ambiguous

D. disinterested

E. objective

5. Which numbered sentence provides an opinion rather than a fact?

A. Sentence 1

B. Sentence 2

C. Sentence 3

D. Sentence 4

E. Sentence 5

6. Which of the following, if true, would best support the argument that the author presents in the passage?

A. Recent research indicates that there has been a rise in antisocial behavior in public places.

B. Statistics reveal that most children would be reluctant to visit relatives who do not allow the use of smart phones while at the table.

C. People who feel addicted to their electronic devices may require psychological counseling.

D. Most people state that they are in control of when and how they use their electronic devices.

E. Most children would rather be outdoors than watch television.

Read the information below and answer the three questions that follow.

Nassir has a busy work schedule and an active social life. His normal work schedule every week is from Monday to Friday, 8 am to 5 pm. Although it is sometimes necessary, he prefers not to work after 5:00 pm as he likes to visit with friends or take part in his hobbies during the evening. A chart of Nassir's commitments for the month of February is shown below.

Sunday	Monday	Tuesday	Wednesday	Thursday	Friday	Saturday
1	2	3 6:00 pm – personal training at gym	4 7:00 pm – meet Ali in town	5 Staff meeting at work – 1:30 pm	6 8:00 pm – Martial arts practice	7
8	9 Work from 1:00 pm to 9:00 pm this week	10 8:30 am – personal training at gym	11 Staff meeting at work – 3:30 pm	12 9:30 am – personal training at gym	13 10:00 am – meet Marta for brunch	14 8:00 am – Go on hike with Martin and Suki
15 5:00 pm – meet Ali in town	16 8:00 pm – meet Terri for a late supper	17 7:00 pm – Martial arts practice	18 8:30 pm – personal training at gym	19 7:30 pm – event at public library	20 6:00 pm – meet Jacinta for coffee	21 Go to Mom and Dad's this weekend
22 2:00 pm – meet Ali in town	23 Work from 1:00 pm to 5:00 pm this week	24 6:30 pm – meet Tom for supper	25 6:00 pm – meet Jacinta for coffee	26 Staff meeting at work – 2:00 pm	27 8:00 am – Martial arts practice	28 10:00 am – Meet Jim for bike ride

7.   Which of the following statements is best supported by the information provided above?

    A. Nassir has staff meetings once a week.

    B. Nassir normally sees his parents once a month.

    C. Nassir finds it difficult to work late in the evening.

    D. Nassir never has to work on Saturday or Sunday.

    E. Nassir writes his work hours on his calendar only when they vary from 8 am to 5 pm.

8.   Based on the information provided above, which of the following statements best explains how Nassir plans the time that he spends exercising?

    A. Nassir's gym is open 24 hours a day, so he can go there any time.

    B. Nassir can go to martial arts practice during the evening only.

    C. Nassir does not like to exercise early in the morning.

    D. Nassir likes to exercise with friends when possible.

    E. Nassir never exercises with Ali in town.

9.   During the month of February, which of the following activities did Nassir take part in at least four times? You may choose more than one answer.

    A. Meeting friends for supper.

    B. Meeting friends for coffee or brunch.

    C. Meeting friends in town.

    D. Personal training at the gym.

    E. Martial arts training.

Read the passage below and answer the four questions that follow.

How is civil order maintained within any given population? The civil order control function suggests that public order is best maintained through agencies other than the police force or militia. Accordingly, martial law, the establishment of military rule over a civilian population, is only imposed when other methods of civil control have proven ineffective. Either the leader of a country's military system or of the country's own government may lay down the edict for the rule of martial law. In the past, this state of affairs most commonly occurred to <u>quell</u> uprisings during periods of colonial occupation or to thwart a coup, defined as an illegal and usually violent seizure of a government by a select group of individuals.

So, how is the declaration of martial law currently regulated? The constitutions of many countries now make provisions for the introduction of martial law, allowing it only in cases of national emergency or in the case of threats to national security from foreign countries. In democratic nations, severe restrictions are imposed on the implementation of martial law, meaning that a formal declaration of military rule over a nation should be rendered virtually impractical. In much the same way, restrictions have been placed on voting in elections in many countries.

10. Which of the following statements gives the best summary of the main point of the lecture?

   A. In the past, the militia was not used to support civil authorities, although it is used this way at present.

   B. In the past, countries did not have constitutions or other established means to regulate the declaration of martial law.

C. There are more threats to national security nowadays than there were in the past.

D. Civil order was more difficult to maintain in the past than it is during the present time.

E. Certain countries have not had to make declarations of martial law in the past.

11. Which of the following is the best meaning of the word quell as it is used in this passage?

A. suppress

B. oppose

C. obliterate

D. militarize

E. bring about

12. What inference about coups can be drawn from the passage?

A. They usually represent a large proportion of the population.

B. They no longer occur as countries now have controls in place to prevent them.

C. They may involve harming government leaders, officials, or citizens.

D. They have taken place most frequently during periods of colonial occupation.

E. Controlling coups is virtually impractical nowadays.

13. Which sentence is least relevant to the main idea of the passage?

   A. The civil order control function suggests that public order is best maintained through agencies other than the police force or militia.

   B. Either the leader of a country's military system or of the country's own government may lay down the edict for the rule of martial law.

   C. The constitutions of many countries now make provisions for the introduction of martial law, allowing it only in cases of national emergency or in the case of threats to national security from foreign countries.

   D. In democratic nations, severe restrictions are imposed on the implementation of martial law, meaning that a formal declaration of military rule over a nation should be rendered virtually impractical.

   E. In much the same way, restrictions have been placed on voting in elections in many countries.

Read the passage below and answer the three questions that follow.

Do mice really prefer cheese to all other foodstuffs? One well-known American exterminator has revealed his secret to catching these pesky rodents: lemon-flavored candy. It appears that the confection has a double advantage. Its sweet smell attracts the mouse much more strongly than does cheese, and its sticky consistency helps to hold the creature captive for the moment it takes for the trap to release.

_____, through logical analogy, we can conclude that it is fallacious to presume that other groups of animals have preferences for certain food groups. _____, we cannot readily conclude that all dogs would choose meat or that all cats would select milk as their favorite foodstuffs.

14. Which of the words or phrases, if inserted in order into the blanks of the passage, would help the reader better understand the progression of the author's argument?
    A. In the same way; Despite this
    B. Therefore; For instance
    C. In this case; On the contrary
    D. On the other hand; Hence
    E. Rather; In effect

15. Which of the following, if true, would fail to support the conclusion that the author makes in the passage?
    A. Mice are attracted more to the texture of the candy than to its smell.
    B. Some animals have a very acute sense of smell.
    C. Many scientific experiments demonstrate that dogs do not prefer the taste and texture of meat to the taste and texture of other food.
    D. Independent observations reveal that mice eat cheese as often as they lemon-flavored candy when both foodstuffs are available to them at the same time.
    E. Quite a few cats are allergic to milk and other dairy products.

16. What is the pattern of organization of the passage?

    A. general to specific

    B. cause and effect

    C. explanation and example

    D. argument and counterargument

    E. theoretical development and new innovations

Read the passage below and answer the three questions that follow.

Ludwig von Beethoven was one of the most influential figures in the development of musical forms during the Classical period. Born in Bonn, Germany, the composer became a professional musician before the age of 12. _____ .

After studying under both Mozart and Haydn, Beethoven became a virtuoso pianist and had many wealthy patrons, who supported him financially. His most popular works are considered to be his fifth and sixth symphonies, and his only opera is entitled *Fidelio*. Listening to any of his creations, it is obvious that that his compositions express the creative energy of the artist himself, rather than being written to suit the demands of his patrons.

17. The main purpose of the passage is to:

    A. suggest that the works of Beethoven, Mozart, and Haydn are very similar.

    B. explore the development of musical composition during the Classical period.

C. provide background information about Beethoven's life and work.

D. explain how Beethoven acquired many wealthy patrons.

E. illustrate the creative energy in Beethoven's symphonies and operas.

18. Which sentence if placed in the line in paragraph 1 would be the most consistent with the writer's purpose and audience?

A. However, certain people do not believe that Beethoven is worthy of such attention.

B. His young age masked a variety of emotional and personal problems.

C. This early started marked the incipience of a very prolific and successful career as a musical artist.

D. On the other hand, other composers were unable to match this level of success.

E. This displayed the trust his parents had placed in him.

19. Which of the following assumptions has most influenced the writer?

A. Beethoven was an incredible, expressive artist.

B. The work of Mozart and Haydn are often overlooked.

C. The German composers were more expressive than those from other countries.

D. Composers would not have been able to write music without their patrons.

E. Patrons wielded too much control over composers.

Read the passage below and answer the four questions that follow.

Today archeologists are still endeavoring to uncover the secrets of Africa's past. Evidence of the earliest human activity has been found in the south and east of the continent, where climatic conditions helped to preserve the human skeletons and stone tools found there. Genetic science confirms that these are quite likely the oldest remains in the world of modern people, with this classification based on the ability of humans to become adaptable and ready to respond to environmental change.

Even though the artifacts and skeletons of early Africans are most commonly found in a highly fragmented state, these findings are more than sufficient in order to make a number of significant conclusions. Perhaps the most important discovery is that there is great <u>variation</u> among the human remains, indicating a wide array of physical differences among members of the population. While the early population was diverse, it has been well established that the earliest species of hominids spread from Africa to other continents

20. Which of the following best describes the organization of the passage?
    A. A common fallacy is described, and then it is refuted.
    B. An unresolved question is posed, and then it is answered.
    C. A problem is described, and then a solution is discussed.
    D. General information about the research is provided, and then the specific findings of the research are presented.
    E. An archeological method is analyzed, and then a contributing phenomenon is discussed.

21.   The author states that "genetic science confirms that these are quite likely the oldest remains in the world of modern people" in paragraph 1 primarily in order to emphasize:

A. the depth and breadth of Africa's history.

B. the way that climatic conditions can help to preserve skeletons.

C. the importance of the stone tools found in African sites.

D. the significance of archeological discoveries in Africa.

E. the fact that human beings are adaptable and responsive.

22.   As used in paragraph 2, the word <u>variation</u> most likely means:

A. distinction

B. discrepancy

C. possibility for error

D. changeability

E. variety

23.   From the passage, it can be inferred that some of the archeological discoveries from Africa:

A. were broken into small pieces or extremely damaged.

B. would not have been located without modern genetic science.

C. were not as important as those from other continents.

D. could not be confirmed by genetic science.

E. were from inhabitants originally from other continents.

Read the passage below and answer the four questions that follow.

A complex series of interactive patterns govern nearly everything the human body does. We eat to a rhythm, and drink, sleep, and even breathe to separate ones. Research shows that the human body clock is affected by the three main rhythmic cycles of the earth, moon, and sun. These rhythms create a sense of time that is both physiological as well as mental. Humans feel hungry about every four hours, sleep about eight hours in every 24-hour period, and dream in cycles of approximately 90 minutes each.

These natural rhythms, sometimes called circadian rhythms, are partially controlled by the hypothalamus in the brain. Circadian rhythms help to explain the "lark vs. owl" hypothesis. Larks are those who quite rightly prefer to rise early in the morning and go to bed early, while owls are those who feel at their best at night and stay up too late. These cycles explain the phenomenon of jet lag, when the individual's body clock is out of step with the actual clock time in his or her new location in the world. In humans, births and deaths also follow predictable cycles, with most births and deaths occurring between midnight and 6:00 am.

24.   In the first paragraph, the author suggests that our mental and physiological sense of time is:

A. appropriate

B. exaggerated

C. oversimplified

D. overgeneralized

E. hypochondriacal

25. In the second to the last sentence of the passage, the phrase "these cycles" refers to:

A. the "lark vs. owl" hypothesis

B. circadian rhythms

C. the hypothalamus in the brain

D. the individual's body clock

E. cycles of birth and death

26. The author's attitude toward owls in the "lark vs. owl" hypothesis can best be described as one of:

A. disapproval

B. skepticism

C. hostility

D. support

E. fanaticism

27. The author would most likely recommend that sufferers of jet lag do which of the following?

A. Better control their circadian rhythms.

B. Take medicine to regulate the hypothalamus.

C. Go to bed earlier than usual.

D. Stay up later than usual.

E. Allow their body clocks to adjust to the time difference naturally.

Read the passage below and answer the three questions that follow.

Depicting the events of a single day, James Joyce's epic novel *Ulysses* took more than 20,000 hours, or a total of eight years, to write. Set in Dublin, the novel was initially published in installments as a series before the Parisian publishing house Shakespeare and Company issued a limited edition of 1,000 copies.

The book was risqué for its time, and was classified as obscene material in the United Stated. After the work was cleared of obscenity charges, an unexpurgated version was accepted for publication by Random House in New York. Ironically, it was not available in Dublin until 40 years later.

28.   From this passage, it seems safe to conclude which of the following?

    A. Irish publishing companies often engage in dilatory practices when dealing with their authors.

    B. Irish publishers were dissuaded in publishing the novel since it depicted the events of only one day.

    C. Random House did not have a division in Dublin at that time.

    D. Social mores in Dublin were much stricter than those of the United States at that time.

    E. Dublin had a more liberal society than that of Paris.

29.   What is the most appropriate title of the passage?

    A. The Life and Work of James Joyce

    B. Problems with James Joyce's *Ulysses*

    C. The Publication of James Joyce's *Ulysses*

D. A Comparative Analysis of the Writings of James Joyce

E. How James Joyce Inspired Young Writers

30. Who is most likely to be the audience of this passage?

A. Young children in an elementary school assembly

B. Authors attending a conference

C. Participants in a workshop for writers

D. College students in a literature lecture

E. Publishers attending a seminar

Read the passage below and answer the four questions that follow.

[1]For every building that is successfully constructed, there are countless others that have never received the chance to leave the drawing board. [2]Some of these unbuilt structures were practical and mundane, while others expressed the flights of fancy of the architect. [3]Known to us today only through the plans left on paper, many unbuilt buildings were originally designed to commemorate particular people or events.

[4]Such was the case with the monument dubbed the *Beacon of Progress*, which was to be erected in Chicago to display exhibits dedicated to great Americans in history. [5]In fact, scholar Samantha Mulholland points out that other proposed projects were even more quixotic, like that of *The Floating Spheres*, described as modules held aloft by hot air to house cities of the future.

31. Samantha Mulholland suggests that which of the following explains why some proposed projects were never constructed?

A. Some projects were never undertaken due to the fact that they did not commemorate any significant event.

B. The plans for some projects had serious design flaws.

C. Some projects were too extravagant and impractical ever to be built.

D. People were not ready to face the future of housing at the time that the construction of *The Floating Spheres* was proposed.

E. *The Floating Spheres* would have been built had it included an important monument.

32. Which numbered sentence from the passage best introduces the writer's main idea?

A. Sentence 1

B. Sentence 2

C. Sentence 3

D. Sentence 4

E. Sentence 5

33. What word best describes the style of writing in this passage?

A. persuasive

B. critical

C. informative

D. condemning

E. neutral

34. Between paragraphs 1 and 2, the writer's approach shifts from:

   A. advantages to disadvantages

   B. cause to effect

   C. general to specific

   D. problem to solution

   E. support to criticism

Read the passage below and answer the three questions that follow.

The ancient legal code of Babylonia had severe sanctions for a wide range of crimes. The consequences of crime were best viewed as a way to express personal vengeance. _____, punishments included cutting off the fingers of boys who had hit their fathers or gouging out the eyes of those who had blinded another person. As with most ancient peoples, the Babylonians did not believe in humane treatments for offenders. They also did not have an advanced system of education in those days.

_____ , Sumerian King Ur Nammu, who formulated a set of laws that were surprisingly modern in their approach, did not follow these draconian forms of retribution. Sumerian law stipulated that perpetrators of violent crimes pay monetary damages to their victims, and Ur Nammu's system is the first recorded example of financial awards being imposed in lieu of other forms of punishment.

35. Which of the words or phrases, if inserted in order into the blanks of the passage, would help the reader better understand the progression of the author's argument?

A. Certainly; In fact

B. Rather; For instance

C. In this case; On the contrary

D. On the other hand; Hence

E. For example; In contrast

36. The author mentions Sumerian King Ur Nammu primarily in order to:

A. criticize previous Babylonian rulers.

B. emphasize the severity of the Babylonian system of justice.

C. imply that Babylonian sanctions were just for their time.

D. point out that humane treatments were not really suitable during that epoch.

E. provide a contrast with the forms of punishment meted out by the Babylonians.

37. Which sentence is least relevant to the main idea of the passage?

A. The ancient legal code of Babylonia had severe sanctions for a wide range of crimes.

B. The consequences of crime were best viewed as a way to express personal vengeance.

C. As with most ancient peoples, the Babylonians did not believe in humane treatments for offenders.

D. They also did not have an advanced system of education in those days.

E. Sumerian law stipulated that perpetrators of violent crimes pay monetary damages to their victims, and Ur Nammu's system is the first recorded example of financial awards being imposed in lieu of other forms of punishment.

Read the passage below and answer the three questions that follow.

In his book *Il Milione*, known in English as *The Travels of Marco Polo*, the intrepid explorer describes the marvels he encountered as he journeyed to China. Upon his visit to the emperor Kublai Khan in Cathay, Polo witnessed the magical illusions performed by the court wizards of the supreme ruler. Polo first saw a row of golden cups levitate over the table as Khan drank from each one without spilling a drop. Next, unrestrained lions would appear to lie down in humility in front of the emperor.

However, Khan was venerated for much more than these acts of mere wizardry. The ruler was also regarded for establishing paper currency, a vast postal system, and a well-maintained network of roads. Some academics have disputed the veracity of Polo's written account of the Khan Empire. However, common sense tells us that there would have been little motive for the explorer to have exaggerated his version of events since he was being held captive at the time with no hope of release.

38.   It can be inferred from the passage that the primary reason why the court wizards performed magical illusions was to:

A. venerate the majesty of Kublai Khan.

B. play a trick on Marco Polo.

C. provide an interesting story for the book *Il Milione.*

D. make Kublai Khan and his court appear powerful and mysterious.

E. help the ruler control wild animals.

39.   Which of the following is the best meaning of the word <u>levitate</u> as it is used in this passage?

A. rise

B. drag

C. hover

D. linger

E. hang up

40.   Which of the following best describes the organization of the passage?

A. It discusses a problem and then provides a solution.

B. It recounts a story and then offers an explanation.

C. It describes a social phenomenon and then illustrates it.

D. It gives the historical background to a piece of writing and then provides further details about it.

E. It compares one version of a historical event to a differing account and interpretation of the event.

Read the passage below and answer the three questions that follow.

Two original forms of theater have emerged from Japanese culture: Noh and Kabuki. Noh, the older form, was originally established to meet the demands of the discriminating Japanese aristocracy and remained unchanged for more than six centuries. Noh renders mundane, everyday activities, like drinking tea or arranging flowers, into exquisite artistic performances. With little spoken dialogue, Noh is classified as more ritual than drama.

Kabuki performances are discernably different than those of Noh. Based on puppet theater, Kabuki is designed to meet the tastes of the general populace, rather than those of the aristocracy. According to long-standing theatrical custom, Kabuki performances can be extremely long, lasting up to twelve hours in some cases. Because of its appeal to the general populace, Kabuki theater remains as fascinating and exotic as it has always been.

41. The passage suggests which of the following about followers of Noh?
     A. They lament the fact that Noh clings on to outdated customs of the past.
     B. They believe that Kabuki theater is overtly flamboyant.
     C. They fear that the popularity of Kabuki theater may diminish the appeal of Noh.

D. They plan to make Noh more up-to-date in order to increase its following.

E. They want to emphasize that followers of Noh are traditional and discerning.

42. The passage implies that Japanese audiences today would respond to Kabuki theater with:

A. admiration

B. impatience

C. confusion

D. boredom

E. detachment

43. Followers of Noh and followers of Kabuki would probably agree with which one of the following statements?

A. Theatrical productions sometimes last too long.

B. Japanese theater is unlikely to change in the future.

C. Theatrical performances should be highly stylized and full of spectacle in order to be effective.

D. Japanese theater is an important and interesting aspect of Japanese culture.

E. Japanese theater has been compromised through exposure to other cultures.

Read the passage below and answer the three questions that follow.

Dance notation for choreography can be based on drawings, stick figures, abbreviations, musical notes, or abstract symbols. _____ _____. In the seventeenth century, Pierre Beauchamp devised a notation system for Baroque dance. Known as Beauchamp-Feuillet notation, his system was used to record dances until the end of the eighteenth century. Later, Vladimir Ivanovich Stepanov, a Russian, was responsible for notating choreographic scores for the famous *Sergevev Ballet Collection*.

Two other notation systems, Labanotation and Benesh notation, also known as choreology, are in wide-spread use today. Apple created the first computerized system to display an animated figure on the screen that illustrated dance moves, and many other software systems have been developed to facilitate computerized dance notation.

44.   According to the passage, Beauchamp-Feuillet notation differs from Vladimir Ivanovich Stepanov's notation system in that Stepanov's system:

A. was used for a different genre of dance during a different time period.

B. was used for works performed in the Russian language.

C. is now computerized.

D. was also known as choreology.

E. did not use animation.

45. Which sentence if placed in the line in paragraph 1 would be the most consistent with the writer's purpose and audience?

A. However, some choreographers regard the use of stick figures as childish and unprofessional.

B. Recording the movements of dance through a shortened series of characters or symbols, more than one hundred systems of dance notation have been created over the past few centuries.

C. As sometimes happens, choreographers cannot read orchestral musical scores.

D. Nevertheless, other innovations in choreography were more significant than dance notation.

E. Dance notation is defined as any system that records the individual movements of a dance.

46. The author most likely mentions Apple and other computerized dance notation systems in the last sentence of the passage in order to:

A. point out the similarities among various computerized systems.

B. advocate the use of computer software for choreographed performances.

C. identify the systems that have replaced choreology.

D. imply that computerized dance notation systems are of better quality than those of the past.

E. indicate possible trends in dance notation.

Read the passage below and answer the two questions that follow.

Known as the Centennial State, Colorado is divided into sixty-three counties. Colorado joined the union as the 38th state in 1876, shortly after the first substantial discovery of gold in the state near Pikes Peak in 1859. The Rocky Mountains run along a north-south line through the center of the state, and there are several other famous national parks and monuments nearby.

Agriculture in the state involves the production of wheat, hay, corn, sugar beets, and other crops, as well as cattle ranching and raising other livestock. However, the packaging, processing, fabrication, and defense industries form the lion's share of revenues from business and commerce in the state.

47.   Which of the following is the best meaning of the words lion's share of as it is used in this passage?

   A. preponderance of

   B. superfluous

   C. excessive

   D. abundant

   E. ever-increasing

48.   The primary purpose of the passage is to:

   A. discuss trade and commerce in a particular state.

   B. sum up the historical background and notable features of a particular state.

C. provide pertinent political details about the acquisition of a particular state.

D. emphasize the importance of agriculture for trade and commerce in Colorado.

E. reveal a surprise fact about a particular state.

Read the passage below and answer the two questions that follow.

The Earth's only natural satellite, the Moon lacks its own atmosphere and is only about one-fourth the size of the planet it orbits. The equality of its orbital rate to that of the Earth is the result of gravitational locking, also known as synchronous rotation. Thus, the same hemisphere of the Moon always faces the earth. Scientific dating of samples from the Moon's crust reveals that the materials range in age from three to four billion years old.

Lunar evolution models suggest that the development of the Moon occurred in five principle stages: (1) increase in mass followed by large-scale melting; (2) separation of the crust with concurrent bombardment by meteors; (3) melting at greater depth; (4) lessening of meteoric bombardment with further melting at depth and the formation of basaltic plains; and (5) the cessation of volcanic activity followed by gradual internal cooling.

49. Which of the following situations best further illustrates the concept of synchronous rotation?

A. The Moon goes through four phases every twenty-eight days.

B. A star appears to shine at the same intensity, regardless of its position in the sky.

C. Two objects fall to the ground at the same speed and land at the same time.

D. An undiscovered planet has two equal hemispheres.

E. A telecommunications satellite is always in the same position above a certain city on Earth.

50. The passage suggests that which one of the following probably occurred after the completion of the process of lunar evolution?

A. Ice continued to melt on the surface of the Moon.

B. The likelihood of the collision of the Moon with a meteor was substantially reduced.

C. Melting at depth still occurred.

D. There were further eruptions of magma or lava.

E The temperature of the internal core of the Moon was lower than it was previously.

ANSWER KEY AND EXPLANATIONS

Practice Reading Test 4

1. The correct answer is B. The primary purpose of the first paragraph is to explain the basic tenets of Marxism, before going on to discuss Marxist views on capitalism and the consequences of private capital. We know this because the second sentence begins with the phrase "according to Marxism." Answer A is too general, and answers C and D are too specific. Answer E is incorrect because the passage talks about Marxism from a political, rather than a historical perspective.

2. The correct answer is D. The first paragraph gives the background to the topic in a general way, and the second paragraph provides specific details about the topic. You may be tempted to choose answer C, but the criticism is only one aspect of the information provided in paragraph 2.

3. The correct answer is E. The writer mentions the "huge impact" that these writings have had on culture and politics in the last sentence in order to juxtapose this impact to Marx's failure to include pragmatic instructions in his work. We know that the author is making a juxtaposition or comparison because the sentence begins with the word "yet ."

4. The correct answer is E. In the second paragraph, the author suggests that the effect of social media on relationships has largely been deleterious, which means harmful. The author asserts that "social media platforms may be having a detrimental impact upon our social skills and interpersonal relationships."

5. The correct answer is E. Sentence 5 states: "Therefore, social media platforms are definitely having a detrimental impact upon our social skills and interpersonal relationships." The word "definitely" indicates that an opinion is being given. We cannot give a definite conclusion because only two studies have been cited in the article. There are certainly other studies that extol the benefits of social media, but the author has decided not to mention these positive aspects of the topic.

6. The correct answer is B. Statistics revealing that most children would be reluctant to visit relatives who do not allow the use of smart phones while at the table would best support the argument presented in the passage. These statistics would support the claim in the passage that "survey results indicate that many people would prefer to interact on Facebook or Twitter, rather than see friends and family in person."

7. The correct answer is E. From the information provided in the chart, we can conclude that Nassir writes his work hours on his calendar only when they vary from 8 am to 5 pm. The facts at the top of the chart tell us that "his normal work schedule every week is from Monday to Friday, 8 am to 5 pm." He has made notes on his calendar for the week beginning on the 9th and the week beginning on the 23rd, so we can surmise that his normal work schedule has been changed for those two weeks.

8. The correct answer is D. From the information provided, we can conclude that Nassir likes to exercise with friends when possible. On the 14th, he is going on a hike with Martin and Suki, and on the 28th he is meeting Jim for a bike ride.

9. The correct answer is D. During the month of February, Nasir will take part in personal training at the gym four times, on the 3rd, 10th, 12th, and 18th of the month.

10. The correct answer is B. The main point of the lecture is that in the past, countries did not have constitutions or other established means to regulate the declaration of martial law. The second paragraph explains that "the constitutions of many countries now make provisions for the introduction of martial law." The use of the word "now" suggests that these provisions were not in place in the past.

11. The correct answer is A. "Quell" means to suppress or conquer.

12. The correct answer is C. The last sentence of the first paragraph states that a coup is "defined as an illegal and usually violent seizure of a government by a select group of individuals." The use of the word "violent" suggests that other people may be harmed or even killed

13. The correct answer is E. The following sentence is least relevant: "In much the same way, restrictions have been placed on voting in elections in many countries." The passage focuses on civil order and martial law. The statement about voting is therefore off-topic.

14. The correct answer is B. The first sentence of paragraph 2 makes a conclusion and the second sentence of paragraph 2 gives an example. So, the best choices are "therefore" and "for instance."

15. The correct answer is D. The passage states: "Through logical analogy, we can therefore conclude that it is fallacious to presume that

other groups of animals have preferences for certain food groups." This conclusion would not be supported if it were true that mice eat cheese as often as they lemon-flavored candy when both foodstuffs are available to them at the same time. If the mice eat both food groups equally, they would not have a preference, and the logical analogy relies upon the existence of this preference.

16. The correct answer is C. The first paragraph explains why the smell and texture of the candy attract mice. The second paragraph gives the case of dogs' food preferences as a further example.

17. The correct answer is C. The primary purpose of the passage is to provide background information about Beethoven's life and work. The passage begins by providing information about the composer's musical training, before going on to talk about his professional life and compositions.

18. The correct answer is C. The words "prolific and successful career" in the new sentence support the ideas of being a professional at a young and of becoming a virtuoso pianist.

19. The correct answer is A. We know that the author has a high regard for the composer because the passage states: "Listening to any of his creations, it is obvious that that his compositions express the creative energy of the artist."

20. The correct answer is D. General information about the research is provided, and then the specific findings of the research are presented. The first paragraph describes the background to archeological research in

Africa, and the second paragraph gives specific details about the remains and artifacts that were discovered there.

21. The correct answer is D. The author states that "genetic science confirms that these are quite likely the oldest remains in the world of modern people" in paragraph 1 primarily in order to emphasize the significance of archeological discoveries in Africa. We know this because the paragraph goes on to explain that "these findings are more than sufficient in order to make a number of significant conclusions."

22. The correct answer is E. As used in paragraph 2, the word "variation" most likely means variety. "Variation" is synonymous with the words "wide array" and "diverse," which are used later in paragraph 2.

23. The correct answer is A. From the passage, it can be inferred that some of the archeological discoveries from Africa were broken into small pieces or extremely damaged. The first sentence of paragraph 2 of the passage tells us that "the artifacts and skeletons of early Africans are most commonly found in a highly fragmented state." "Fragmented" means broken into pieces.

24. The correct answer is A. In the first paragraph, the author suggests that our mental and physiological sense of time is appropriate. The author explains that all human beings have this sense of time. The author does not criticize this behavior, but rather, provides factual information about the topic. From the tone of the passage, we can therefore surmise that that author views this behavior as appropriate.

25. The correct answer is B. In the second to the last sentence of the passage, the phrase "these cycles" refers to circadian rhythms. The two previous sentences state: "Circadian rhythms help to explain the "lark vs. owl" hypothesis. Larks are those who quite rightly prefer to rise early in the morning and go to bed early, while owls are those who feel at their best at night and stay up too late." Larks and owls are given as an example, so the phrase "these rhythms" refers back to the subject of circadian rhythms in the previous sentence.

26. The correct answer is A. The author's attitude toward owls in the "lark vs. owl" hypothesis can best be described as one of disapproval. The author says that larks "quite rightly prefer to rise early in the morning," but owls "stay up too late." So, the author disapproves of the owl's behavior.

27. The correct answer is E. The author would most likely recommend that sufferers of jet lag allow their body clocks to adjust to the time difference naturally. The author begins the second paragraph by explaining that "these natural rhythms, sometimes called circadian rhythms, are partially controlled by the hypothalamus in the brain." Since the author refers to the rhythms as a natural phenomenon, he or she would most likely suggest that the time difference be overcome naturally.

28. The correct answer is D. We can make this conclusion because the author suggests that social mores in Dublin were much stricter than those of the United States at the time that *Ulysses* was published in New York. The passage tells us that "the book was risqué for its time" and was originally classified as "obscene material." In this context, the word "mores" means moral views, and the word "risqué" means indecent.

29. The correct answer is C. Paragraph 1 uses the words "published" and "publishing," while paragraph 2 uses the word "publication." So, the best title is "The Publication of James Joyce's *Ulysses.*"

30. The correct answer to D. This would likely be introductory material in a literary lecture because the passage gives some basic background to the book. The passage does offer any advice that would be relevant to writers, authors, or publishers.

31. The correct answer is C. Samantha Mulholland suggests some proposed projects were never constructed because they were too extravagant and impractical ever to be built. The passage states: "Scholar Samantha Mulholland points out other proposed projects were far more quixotic." The word "quixotic" means extravagant and impractical.

32. The correct answer is A. The rest of the passage talks about buildings that "never received the chance to leave the drawing board."

33. The correct answer is C. The passage merely provides information. It does not try to persuade, nor does it give any opinions.

34. The correct answer is C. Paragraph 1 gives the general background to the topic, while paragraph 2 gives two specific examples of unbuilt structures.

35. The correct answer is E. The third sentence of paragraph 1 gives an example of a punishment. The first sentence of paragraph 2 contrasts these punishments to a different set of laws. So, the best answers are "for example" and "in contrast."

36. The correct answer is E. The author mentions Sumerian King Ur Nammu primarily in order to provide a contrast with the usual forms of punishment meted out by the Babylonians. The passage states that "the Babylonians did not believe in humane treatments for offenders." However, King Ur Nammu "did not follow these draconian forms of retribution."

37. The correct answer is D. The passage is describing laws, so the comment about education is not relevant.

38. The correct answer is D. It can be inferred from the passage that the primary reason why the court wizards performed magical illusions was to make Kublai Khan and his court appear powerful and mysterious. The first paragraph uses the words "amazement" and "astonishing" to express the mysteriousness of the court.

39. The correct answer is C. The author most probably uses the word "levitate" in paragraph 1 to mean hover. The words "levitate" and "hover" both mean to be suspended in midair.

40. The correct answer is D. The passage gives the historical background to a piece of writing and then provides further details about it. Paragraph 1 describes the book *Il Milione*, and paragraph 2 provides some additional information about Polo's written account of events.

41. The correct answer is E. The passage suggests that the followers of Noh are traditional, discerning, and serious. Paragraph 1 states that Noh is for the "discriminating Japanese aristocracy." The word "aristocracy"

indicates that the dance is traditional in nature, while the word "discriminating" means "discerning."

42. The correct answer is A. The second paragraph implies that Japanese audiences today would respond to Kabuki theater with admiration. The last sentence of the second paragraph states: "Because of its appeal to the general populace, Kabuki theater remains as fascinating and exotic as it has always been." We can surmise that people probably admire something that fascinates them.

43. The correct answer is D. Followers of Noh and followers of Kabuki would probably agree that Japanese theater is an important and interesting aspect of Japanese culture. The first sentence of the passage explains that these forms of theater "have emerged from Japanese culture." Since an article has been devoted to this topic, we can assume that followers consider the topic to be an important and interesting aspect of the Japanese culture.

44. The correct answer is A. According to the passage, Beauchamp-Feuillet notation differs from Vladimir Ivanovich Stepanov's notation system in that Stepanov's system was used for a different genre of dance during a different time period. Stepanov's system was used for ballet after the eighteenth century. The system that Pierre Beauchamp devised was used for Baroque dance until the end of the eighteenth century.

45. The correct answer is B. The phrase "past few centuries" in the new sentence provides a link to the historical background provided in the next paragraph. You may be tempted to choose answer choice E, which offers

a definition. However, answer choice B is better because it has both a definition and the chronological connection.

46. The correct answer is E. The author most likely mentions Apple and other computerized dance notation systems in the last sentence of the passage in order to indicate possible trends in dance notation. We know this because the sentence focuses on new developments in dance notation.

47. The correct answer is A. The phrase "preponderance of" could be substituted for "lion's share of" in the second paragraph with the least change in meaning. Both phrases refer to the majority of something.

48. The correct answer is B. The primary purpose of the passage is to sum up the historical background and notable features of a particular state. The other answer choices provide specific details from the passage, rather than the primary purpose.

49. The correct answer is E. The concept of synchronous rotation is illustrated in the situation in which a telecommunications satellite is always in the same position above a certain city on Earth. This is similar to the way in which the same hemisphere of the Moon always faces the earth.

50. The correct answer is E. Point 5 in paragraph 2 states that the last step in lunar evolution was "the cessation of volcanic activity followed by gradual internal cooling." So, we can conclude that after lunar evolution, the temperature of the internal core of the Moon was lower than it was previously.

Made in the USA
Las Vegas, NV
01 December 2023